Euthanasia and Assisted Suicide

ISSUES

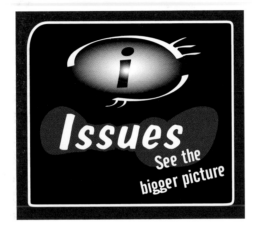

Volume 217

Series Editor

Lisa Firth

Independence

Educational Publishers

Cambridge

First published by Independence

The Studio, High Green

Great Shelford

Cambridge CB22 5EG

England

© Independence 2011

British Library Cataloguing in Publication Data

Euthanasia and assisted suicide. -- (Issues ; v. 217)

1. Euthanasia--Moral and ethical aspects. 2. Right to die.

3. Assisted suicide--Moral and ethical aspects.

I. Series II. Firth, Lisa.

179.7-dc23

ISBN-13: 978 1 86168 597 1

Printed in Great Britain

MWL Print Group Ltd

CONTENTS

Chapter 1 The Ethical Debate

Chapter 2 Legal Issues and Implications

OTHER TITLES IN THE ISSUES SERIES

For more on these titles, visit: www.independence.co.uk

A note on critical evaluation

Because the information reprinted here is from a number of different sources, readers should bear in mind the origin of the text and whether the source is likely to have a particular bias when presenting information (just as they would if undertaking their own research). It is hoped that, as you read about the many aspects of the issues explored in this book, you will critically evaluate the information presented. It is important that you decide whether you are being presented with facts or opinions. Does the writer give a biased or an unbiased report? If an opinion is being expressed, do you agree with the writer?

Euthanasia and Assisted Suicide offers a useful starting point for those who need convenient access to information about the many issues involved. However, it is only a starting point. Following each article is a URL to the relevant organisation's website, which you may wish to visit for further information.

Euthanasia

Information from Politics.co.uk.

What is euthanasia?

Euthanasia comes from Greek, meaning 'pleasant death'. It typically refers to the killing of a person for their own (or another) good, usually to end their suffering.

While virtually no-one in modern society would condone involuntary euthanasia, 'mercy killings' and 'assisted suicides', where the person killed consents to his or her fate, are the subject of heated international debate.

An important distinction in UK law exists between active euthanasia and passive euthanasia. Since the Bland ruling of 1993, 'assisted suicides', which involve 'omissions' that are principally the removal of life-saving care, are not illegal. However, actively taking action to end another's life is illegal, even with consent.

Medically assisted suicide, where doctors help patients to die or actually kill them, is legal in a number of European countries, including Belgium and the Netherlands.

Euthanasia is a highly complex issue involving difficult questions regarding the role of modern government and the rights of individual citizens. The central premise of those supporting legalisation of euthanasia is the right of individuals, often in unbearable pain, to choose where and when they will die. The arguments against the legalisation of euthanasia highlight the utilitarian role of governance and the inability of any government to support acts violating the right to life of its citizens.

Background

In law, euthanasia has no special legal position in the UK. Instances described as euthanasia are treated as murder or manslaughter. However, the Suicide Act 1961 makes a specific offence of 'criminal liability for complicity in another's suicide', while declaring suicide itself to be legal.

In practice, however, the prosecution of euthanasia in the UK is distinct from other cases of unlawful killing – the consent of the Attorney General to prosecute is an explicit requirement of the Act, and sentencing is influenced by the often desperate and harrowing circumstances of individual cases.

The law has been reviewed since 1961, but has not been substantially changed, despite regular attempts by backbenchers in Parliament.

Euthanasia is a highly complex issue involving difficult questions regarding the role of modern government and the rights of individual citizens

---

Since the Human Rights Act 1998, however, campaigners have claimed that the denial of a right to release oneself from unbearable pain amounts to inhuman and degrading treatment (Article 3 of the European Convention on Human Rights), is a violation of privacy and family life (Article 8), amounts to discrimination given the legality of suicide itself, and that an individual's inherent dignity and 'right to die' is violated by the current legislation.

Jurisprudence, however, does not recognise a parallel right to die implied by the right to life.

Controversies

The subject of euthanasia is a highly controversial and divisive topic, raising an array of sophisticated moral, ethical, social, philosophical, legal and religious concerns.

Many of these were aired in the case of Diane Pretty, who was dying of motor neurone disease and wanted her husband to end her life without being prosecuted for aiding and abetting suicide. Her case led to a high-profile legal and public debate on the issue, as her husband first applied to domestic courts (up to the House of Lords), and then to the European Court of Human Rights (ECHR) for judicial review of the refusal to give him immunity from prosecution. Had the case been successful, it would have effectively struck down the legal ban on assisted suicide.

Mrs Pretty was unsuccessful because the domestic courts, in recognition of the complex moral considerations

at stake, deferred to the democratic will of Parliament as enshrined in the legal text. The ECHR applied the EU equivalent, the 'Margin of Appreciation', and rescinded from passing judgement on the issue in 2002.

There are two main groups of arguments deployed against euthanasia.

The first group is religious: many religions, notably Christianity, do not recognise a right to die, believing life to be a divine gift. Christians also regard suicide as a sin.

The second group relates to the requirement of consent. The capacity of a terminally-ill patient to give informed consent for their own killing is questioned. It is also suggested that doctors and relatives may press people into accepting euthanasia against their will and for reasons not related to their welfare.

Many religions, notably Christianity, do not recognise a right to die

In the US, Dr Jack Kevorkian – known as 'Dr Death' – successfully challenged the law on euthanasia, avoiding prosecution for conducting medically-assisted suicides across the country for ten years. In a landmark 1999 decision, however, he was sent to prison for ten to 25 years for administering a lethal injection.

Lord Joel Joffe has been campaigning since 2003 to allow assisted dying for the terminally ill. His Private Members' Bill 'Patient (Assisted Dying)' was introduced to the House of Lords in February of that year.

In November 2004, Lord Joffe's new 'Assisted Dying for the Terminally Ill Bill' to legalise assisted dying received its first reading in the House of Lords and in November 2005 an amended version of the Bill was introduced to the Lords. But in May 2006, following a highly publicised seven-hour debate, peers voted by 148 to 100 to reject the Bill.

The ongoing campaigns to legalise euthanasia or assisted dying, some of which are attracting the support of various celebrities, have raised particular concerns amongst people with disabilities and their families and supporters. They fear the calls for legalisation will intensify and say they feel particularly vulnerable in the current economic climate with cuts in vital public services on which they depend.

Now the disabilities group Not Dead Yet UK (NDYUK) has launched its own Resistance Campaign and is calling on all MPs to sign the 'Resistance Charter 2010' declaring that they will support palliative care and independent living services and maintain legal protection for all people who are terminally ill or disabled.

Statistics

Countries which have enacted legislation on assisted dying:

Belgium – The Belgian Act on Euthanasia was passed in May 2002. The law allows adults who are in a 'futile medical condition of constant and unbearable physical or mental suffering that cannot be alleviated' to request voluntary euthanasia.

Luxembourg – In February 2008, the Luxembourg Parliament approved a Law on the Right to Die with Dignity. This allows a person who is suffering unbearably from an illness, and is mentally competent, to request medical assistance to die.

The Netherlands – The Netherlands introduced assisted dying legislation in 2002. Patients who have an incurable condition, face unbearable suffering and are mentally competent may be eligible for voluntary euthanasia or assisted dying.

Oregon (USA) – The Oregon Death with Dignity Act has been in place for ten years. It gives terminally ill, mentally competent people the option of an assisted death.

Switzerland – Voluntary euthanasia is forbidden in Switzerland. However, Article 115 of the Swiss Penal Code exempts people who assist someone to commit suicide, if they act with entirely honourable motives.

Source: Dignity in Dying – 2011

Quotes

'I believe that decisions about the timing and manner of death belong to the individual as a human right. I believe it is wrong to withhold medical methods of terminating life painlessly and swiftly when an individual has a rational and clear-minded sustained wish to end his or her life.'

Professor A C Grayling, Dignity in Dying Patron

'Disabled and terminally ill people fear that calls to legalise assisted suicide and euthanasia are likely to intensify. Our concerns are heightened by the current economic climate and calls from politicians from all parties for cuts in public services.

'We, and our families, rely upon such services to live with dignity.... We face a bleak situation as calls for assisted suicide to be lawful are renewed, whilst vital services are being withdrawn or denied.'

NDYUK's 'Resistance Charter 2010: Protecting the lives of disabled & terminally ill people.'

⇨ The above information is reprinted with kind permission from Politics.co.uk. Visit www.politics.co.uk for more information.

© Politics.co.uk

POLITICS.CO.UK

Arguments for and against euthanasia

Below are some of the main arguments used by both supporters and opponents of euthanasia and assisted suicide. None of these arguments necessarily represent the opinions or policies of NHS Choices or the Department of Health.

Arguments for euthanasia and assisted suicide

There are several main types of argument used to support the practices of euthanasia and assisted suicide:

⇨ An ethical argument: according to the widely accepted ethical principle of respect for autonomy (freedom of choice), people should have the right to control their own body and life (as long as they do not abuse any other person's rights), and the state should not create laws that prevent citizens being able to choose when and how they die.

⇨ A pragmatic argument: euthanasia, especially passive euthanasia, is already a widespread practice (allegedly), just not one that people are willing to confess to, so surely it is better to properly regulate euthanasia.

The pragmatic argument is discussed in more depth below.

Pragmatic argument

The pragmatic argument states that many of the practices used in end-of-life care are essentially a type of euthanasia in all but name.

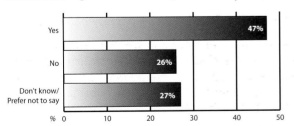

If you had a terminal disease for which there is no possible cure would you personally consider the option of assisted suicide, travelling abroad if necessary?

- Yes: 47%
- No: 26%
- Don't know/Prefer not to say: 27%

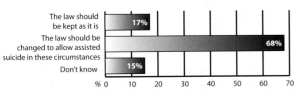

Do you think British law should be kept as it is, or should be changed so that people with incurable diseases have the right to ask close friends or relatives to help them commit suicide, without those friends or relatives risking prosecution?

- The law should be kept as it is: 17%
- The law should be changed to allow assisted suicide in these circumstances: 68%
- Don't know: 15%

Base: 2853 GB adults; Fieldwork: 19-20 July 2011;
Source: Assisted suicide laws, © YouGov plc. (www.yougov.com)

For example, there is the practice of making a 'Do Not Attempt Resuscitation' (DNAR) order, where a person has requested that they do not receive treatment if their heart stops beating or they stop breathing.

Critics have argued that DNAR is essentially a type of passive euthanasia as a person is being denied treatment that could potentially save their life.

Another controversial practice is known as palliative sedation. This is when a person experiencing extreme suffering, for which there is no effective treatment, is put to sleep using sedative medication. For example, palliative sedation is often used to treat burns victims who are expected to die.

While palliative sedation is not directly carried out for the purpose of ending lives, many of the sedatives used carry a risk of shortening a person's lifespan. So it could be argued that palliative sedation is a type of active euthanasia.

So the pragmatic argument is that if euthanasia is essentially being performed anyway, society might as well properly legalise and regulate euthanasia.

It should be stressed that the interpretations of DNAR and palliative sedation presented above are extremely controversial and certainly not accepted by most doctors, nurses and palliative care specialists. See *Alternatives to euthanasia and assisted suicide* on page 13 for responses to these interpretations.

Arguments against euthanasia and assisted suicide

There are four main types of argument used by people who are opposed to euthanasia and assisted suicide.

⇨ The religious argument: these practices can never be justified for religious reasons, for example many people believe that only God has the right to end a human life.

⇨ The 'slippery slope' argument: this is based on the concern that legalising euthanasia could lead to significant unintended changes in our healthcare system and society at large that we would later come to regret.

⇨ The medical ethics argument: asking doctors, nurses or any other health professional to carry out acts of euthanasia or assist in a suicide would be a violation of fundamental medical ethics.

➡ The alternative argument: there is no reason a person should suffer either mentally or physically as there are effective end-of-life treatments available, so euthanasia is not a valid treatment option but instead represents a failure on the part of the doctor involved in a person's care.

Religious argument

The most common religious argument is that human beings are the sacred creation of God, so human life is by extension sacred. This means there are limits to what humans can do with their life, such as ending it.

Only God should choose when a human life ends, so committing an act of euthanasia or assisting in suicide is acting against the will of God and is sinful.

This argument, or variations on it, is shared by the Christian, Jewish and Islamic faiths.

The issue is more complex in Hinduism and Buddhism. A number of scholars from both faiths have argued that euthanasia and assisted suicides are ethically acceptable acts in some circumstances, but these views do not have universal support among Hindus and Buddhists.

'Slippery slope' argument

The 'slippery slope' argument is based on the idea that once a healthcare service, and by extension the Government, starts killing its own citizens, a line is crossed that should have never been crossed and a dangerous precedent has been set.

The concern is that a society that allows voluntary euthanasia will then gradually change its attitudes

to include non-voluntary and then involuntary euthanasia.

Also, legalised voluntary euthanasia could eventually lead to a wide range of unforeseen consequences, such as the following:

➡ Very ill people who need constant care or people with severe disabilities may feel pressured to request euthanasia so they are not a burden to their family.

➡ Legalising euthanasia may discourage research into palliative treatments and possibly cures for people with terminal illnesses.

➡ Doctors may occasionally be badly mistaken about a patient's diagnosis and outlook and the patient may choose euthanasia as they have been wrongly told they have a terminal condition.

Medical ethics argument

The medical ethics argument states that legalising euthanasia would violate one of the most important medical ethics, which in the words of the International Code of Medical Ethics is: 'A doctor must always bear in mind the obligation of preserving human life from conception'.

Asking doctors to abandon their obligation to preserve human life could fatally damage the doctor–patient relationship. Doctors could become hardened to death and the process of causing death becomes a routine administrative task. This could lead to a lack of compassion when dealing with elderly, disabled or terminally-ill patients.

In turn, people with complex health needs or severe disabilities could become distrustful of their doctor's efforts and intentions, thinking their doctor would rather 'kill them off' than take responsibility for a complex and demanding case.

Alternative argument

The alternative argument is that, because of advances in palliative care and mental health treatment, there is no reason any person should ever feel they are suffering intolerably, whether it is physical or mental suffering or both.

According to this argument, if the right care and environment is provided, there is no reason a person cannot have a dignified and painless natural death.

September 2010

➡ Reproduced by kind permission of the Department of Health. Please visit www.nhs.uk for more information on this and other related topics.

© Crown Copyright – nhs.uk

A humanist discussion of euthanasia

Information from the British Humanist Association.

What is euthanasia? Some definitions

⇨ Euthanasia originally meant 'a gentle and easy death', and is now used to mean 'the act of inducing an easy death', usually referring to acts which terminate or shorten life painlessly in order to end suffering where there is no prospect of recovery.

⇨ Voluntary euthanasia, sometimes called 'assisted suicide', is used in cases where the sufferer has made it clear that s/he wishes to die and has requested help to bring this about.

⇨ Involuntary euthanasia occurs when no consent or wish to die is expressed by the sufferer. To define this type further:

↳ Non-voluntary euthanasia – where patients cannot express a wish to die (patients in comas, infants, cases of extreme senile dementia, those who cannot communicate for other reasons);

↳ Involuntary euthanasia – where patients can express a wish to die but don't (this equates to murder).

The way in which the euthanasia is carried out can also be defined:

⇨ Active, or direct, euthanasia involves specific actions (e.g. lethal drugs or injections) intended to bring about death. This is illegal in Great Britain.

⇨ Passive euthanasia is the practice, widely carried out and generally judged to be legal, where patients are allowed to die, by withdrawing treatment and/or nourishment. A common practice of this is a patient signing a 'Do Not Resuscitate' (DNR) document.

⇨ Indirect euthanasia (sometimes referred to as 'the double effect') is the practice of providing treatment, normally pain relief, which has the side-effect of hastening death. This is also widely practised and generally considered legal if killing was not the intention.

The problem

Arguments about euthanasia often hinge on the 'right to life' and the 'right to die'. The first is a widely accepted basic human right and moral value, based on the fact that people generally want to live. But what should we do when seriously ill people no longer want to live? Do they have a right to die? Sufferers sometimes wish to commit suicide but do not have the physical strength or the means to do it painlessly.

Like many problems of medical ethics, this has become more pressing recently. A century ago, most people died quite quickly (and probably painfully) if they had serious injuries or illnesses. Nowadays they can be treated, sometimes cured, and often kept alive almost indefinitely. Codes of conduct formulated centuries ago, for example those found in sacred texts, or the Hippocratic oath, cannot necessarily help us with 21st-century problems of medical ethics.

Some views on euthanasia

Humanists think that in a lot of circumstances voluntary euthanasia is the morally right course of action to take. Many religious people, however, think that euthanasia is always morally wrong, regardless of whether the suffering person really wants to die.

In order to decide which approach one takes to the issue, it is helpful to consider some of the common arguments made against voluntary euthanasia:

The 'slippery slope' argument

The 'slippery slope' or 'thin end of the wedge' argument says that if you permit voluntary euthanasia, involuntary euthanasia will follow.

Hitler's programme of euthanasia is often cited, wherein the Nazis used 'humane' excuses to exterminate mentally and physically disabled patients during the Holocaust. This analogy might be cited to support two types of argument against legalising voluntary euthanasia:

⇨ a logical argument – that it is impossible to discriminate between unjustified and justified cases of euthanasia;

⇨ a psychological argument – that a policy of euthanasia could erode the psychological barriers against killing and lead to unjustified killings.

To the analogy itself, humanists would say that this was clearly involuntary euthanasia carried out by a murderous dictator who did not begin by offering voluntary euthanasia to terminally ill hospital patients who had requested it. There was no 'slippery slope' involved, so analogy to Hitler's euthanasia is a straw man. Humanists also reject the logical argument, arguing that the boundary between voluntary and involuntary euthanasia is a very distinct one and not difficult to maintain. Typical cases, like that of Diane Pretty, demonstrate that most of the time it is very clear that it is the patient making the choice for him/herself. The psychological argument is also viewed by the humanist as implausible since there is no reason to believe that passing a law on voluntary euthanasia

would demean other laws concerning death, such as murder. Assisting a terminally ill person to die who has expressively asked for it is very different from killing an innocent victim.

'Playing God'

Religious people often argue that it is not for doctors to 'play God' and that it's for God to decide when people die. But by this logic it must be said that all medical interventions are 'playing God'; although most religious people undergo vaccinations which keep them alive longer than 'God' planned and do not consider this immoral. The humanist thinks we have to decide for ourselves how we use medical powers. Also, humanists do not believe that the manner and time of death are for a deity to decide and/or that interference in the course of nature is unacceptable. Arguments which invoke God are unconvincing to those who do not believe in gods, and laws should not be based on claims which rely on religious faith.

Euthanasia originally meant 'a gentle and easy death', and is now used to mean 'the act of inducing an easy death'

The sanctity of life

Religious people also often use phrases like 'the sanctity of life' to justify the view that life has intrinsic value and must not be destroyed. Humanists, too, see a special value in human life, but think that if an individual has decided on rational grounds that his life has lost its meaning and value, that evaluation should be respected.

The 'doing' and 'allowing' distinction

Some religious people maintain that there is a moral distinction between acts which cause death (active euthanasia) and omissions which cause death (passive euthanasia), only the second being morally permissible.

Many humanists think they've got it the wrong way round, because the first is quicker and thus kinder for everyone involved, though both are probably painless for the patient.

Many of the medical profession and politicians have also accepted this traditional distinction. It might be easier for doctors to withdraw or withhold treatment than it would be for them to administer a lethal drug – but this does not necessarily make it right. It would be wrong to force doctors and nurses to do things that they consider morally wrong, but patients wishing for assistance in dying should be allowed to seek a doctor who will help them.

The effects on others

Some think that suicide is wrong because of the great pain it often causes to those left behind. If one believes suicide is wrong, then assisted suicide, seemingly, must be wrong too.

But the death of a terminally ill and suffering patient would probably be a merciful release for everyone involved and so is very different in its effects from other suicides.

The humanist view

Humanists are non-religious people who live by moral principles based on reason and respect for others, not obedience to dogmatic rules. They promote happiness and fulfilment in this life because they believe it is the only one we have. Humanist concern for quality of life and respect for personal autonomy lead to the view that in many circumstances voluntary euthanasia is the morally right course.

People should have the right to choose a painless and dignified end, either at the time or beforehand, perhaps in a 'living will'. The right circumstances might include: extreme pain and suffering; helplessness and loss of personal dignity; permanent loss of those things which have made life worth living for this individual. To postpone the inevitable with no intervening benefit is not a moral act.

Individuals should be allowed to decide on such personal matters for themselves; if someone in possession of full information and sound judgement decides that her continued life has no value, her wishes should be respected.

While humanists generally support voluntary euthanasia, they also uphold the need for certain safeguards. These may include counselling, the prevention of pressure on patients, clear witnessed instructions from the patient, the involvement of several doctors, no reasonable hope of recovery – measures which would prevent involuntary euthanasia.

There is no rational moral distinction between allowing someone to die and actively assisting them to die in these circumstances: the intention and the outcome (the death of the patient) are the same in both cases, but the more active means is probably the more compassionate one. The BHA supports attempts to reform the current law on voluntary euthanasia.

⇨ The above information is reprinted with kind permission from the British Humanist Association. Visit www.humanismforschools.org.uk for more information.

© British Humanist Association

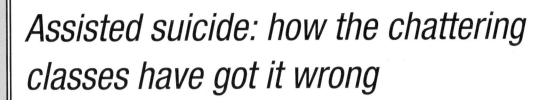

Assisted suicide: how the chattering classes have got it wrong

Information from the Centre for Policy Studies.

By Cristina Odone

A painless and speedy death, resulting from a hygienic medical procedure that leaves no mess: assisted suicide is the final consumer fantasy. Although illegal in Britain, it is already available to the determined and comfortably-off, who can buy (at £10,000 a shot) an appointment with death at the Dignitas clinic in Switzerland. Here, completely legally, a physician will inject them with a fatal poison. Why can't, argue the distinguished and articulate advocates of assisted suicide and voluntary euthanasia, this choice be available to all?

The simple answer is that, if we legalise assisted suicide, we risk having a strident élite condemning the less fortunate to a premature death. For it is the marginalised, the disabled, the less articulate and the poor who are most likely to be under pressure to accelerate their death. The NHS hospital or care home, engulfed by a rising tide of elderly people, and starved of funds, will feel the burden of the 'bed-blocker' – and fill the insecure and vulnerable patient with guilt for taxing a system that is already under severe strain. Above all, the disadvantaged, fearful of authorities and lost in bureaucracy, may not know how to manipulate the system and may, in comparison to the confident members of the choice-obsessed consumerist élite, be more subject to manipulation by others.

A well-organised lobby of euthanasia supporters, led by Dignity in Dying, have tried to convince us that legalising assisted suicide is the most humane solution for everyone's final exit. Their campaign draws its force not only from the worried well, but also from new, and alarming, demographic forecasts: by 2033, 23% of the population will be over the age of 65. Research undertaken by Barbara Gomes and Professor Irene Higginson suggests that the annual number of deaths is expected to rise by 17% between 2012 and 2030.

This huge new pressure on our health and support systems risks turning our last stage of life, and our death, into a nightmare. There are two dangers: the first is that the needs of those too old and weak to look after themselves may be ignored; the other is that when everyone is competing for limited resources, the aged may feel guilty because they are diverting investments from everyone else.

The legalisation of assisted suicide and voluntary euthanasia was once thought unthinkable in this country, where it was associated with the Nazis' secret euthanasia programme. Yet public demand for what is being euphemistically called the 'right to die' has grown hugely (to 74%, according to a poll last year by *The Times*). Cases such as Lynne Gilderdale's, who had suffered with a paralysing form of ME for 17 years until her mother, Bridget Kathleen Gilderdale, helped her to die by giving her an overdose, have triggered sympathetic reactions; their prosecution has met with huge opposition.

The issue has been debated in Parliament four times over the past six years. Debbie Purdy, who has MS, last

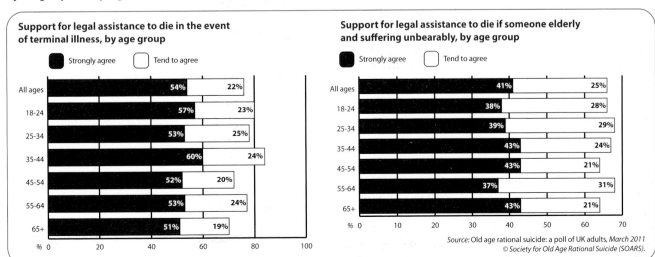

Support for legal assistance to die in the event of terminal illness, by age group

■ Strongly agree □ Tend to agree

	Strongly agree	Tend to agree
All ages	54%	22%
18-24	57%	23%
25-34	53%	25%
35-44	60%	24%
45-54	52%	20%
55-64	53%	24%
65+	51%	19%

% 0   20   40   60   80   100

Support for legal assistance to die if someone elderly and suffering unbearably, by age group

■ Strongly agree □ Tend to agree

	Strongly agree	Tend to agree
All ages	41%	25%
18-24	38%	28%
25-34	39%	29%
35-44	43%	24%
45-54	43%	21%
55-64	37%	31%
65+	43%	21%

% 0   10   20   30   40   50   60   70

Source: Old age rational suicide: a poll of UK adults, March 2011
© *Society for Old Age Rational Suicide (SOARS).*

year won the right to have the prosecution guidelines affecting those who assist suicide clarified. Keir Starmer QC, the Director of Public Prosecutions (DPP), published his guidelines in February 2010.

The new guidelines have not paved the way for assisted suicide; they call for each case to be judged on its own merits. But those working with the elderly, the disabled and the terminally ill worry that, once introduced on compassionate grounds, assisted suicide will lead to death on request or euthanasia without consent.

In particular, they contend that any change in the law will expose the vulnerable to coercion by their family or other interested parties, such as a doctor, or a nursing home director. They are concerned that too many could be talked or pressured into giving up their lives for the convenience of younger, healthier individuals.

For the real battle over assisted suicide and euthanasia is between the haves and have-nots. Euthanasia enthusiasts such as Lord Joffe and Lord Falconer (both of whom have attempted in Parliament to legalise assisted suicide) and Dignity in Dying patrons such as Terry Pratchett, A N Wilson and Patricia Hewitt need not fear coercion if assisted suicide becomes legal: articulate, determined and well-connected, they would know how to protect themselves in any situation. But for millions of others, too anxious, inarticulate or fragile to clearly defend their needs, their disadvantage may cost them their lives. As Dr Carol J. Gill has written:

'Viewing the world from a position of privilege may limit one's insight into the consequences of a policy change whose greatest impact could fall on socially marginalised groups.'

The debate about assisted suicide and euthanasia has been portrayed as a battle between religious and anti-religious groups. It is not. Many secularists view assisted suicide and euthanasia with horror; while there are believers who regard assisting someone to end their lives to be an act of charity. Out of the 93 speeches dedicated to this issue in Hansard, only six are by bishops; the rest are by parliamentarians concerned that a change in the law carries with it the potential for coercion.

If this is to be resolved, it should be on the basis of facts, not faith. Legalising assisted suicide risks harming the most vulnerable. It should be rejected on grounds of public safety, not personal morality.

The dangers inherent in the legalisation of assisted suicide can be grouped into four categories:

Second-class human beings

The danger is that less-than-perfect citizens will be deemed expendable. Not only will those who require a great deal of care and assistance, including the elderly, feel that in the new hierarchy promoted by euthanasia they stand at the bottom rung; they may feel guilty, seeing themselves reduced to a burden on their families or the state. This will be all the truer of the socially marginalised.

Doctor Death

When the doctor prescribes a fatal potion or administers a lethal injection, rather than battling to save you from disease and/or death, trust in doctor–patient relationships risks being destroyed. It is precisely because we trust our doctors always to act in our best interests that what is being euphemistically called 'assisted dying' is so dangerous: a doctor who agreed to a patient's request to 'end it all' could all too easily send a signal, however unintended, that the doctor considered death was the best course of action in the patient's circumstances.

The death squad

Who will regulate these deaths, if we don't adopt the physician-assisted suicide model? Assuming we allow for conscientious objectors, a self-selecting cadre of 'death regulators' will take charge of assisted suicide. Who will be able to check this all-powerful death squad? Who can be sure that at the last minute the patient does not undergo a change of heart yet is pushed to go ahead with suicide anyway by those present? None of the scenarios put forward by the euthanasia lobby offer any insurance that coercion will not take place once official approval for an assisted suicide has been given.

Slippery slope

Once assisted suicide becomes legal, it will slide into voluntary euthanasia, which in turn will lead to involuntary euthanasia. Physician-assisted suicide is, after all, simply physician-administered euthanasia. Once the principle is breached that a doctor may act knowingly to bring about a patient's death, the way to full-scale euthanasia lies open.

In short, legalising euthanasia will change our lives, forever. Our world will become a harder, more selfish place, where the weak will have no voice and no value. The Government must therefore resist calls for the legalisation of assisted suicide and voluntary euthanasia.

October 2010

⇨ The above information is reprinted with kind permission from the Centre for Policy Studies. Visit www.cps.org.uk for more information on this and related topics.

© Centre for Policy Studies

The slippery slope argument

Information from The World Federation of Right to Die Societies.

Background on the slippery slope argument

Much of the opposition to the legalisation of assisted dying is based on the fear that voluntary requests from patients for physician aid in dying would soon be expanded to allow for patients to make advance directives for euthanasia upon the meeting of particular physical conditions. It would then be further expanded to decisions for euthanasia being made by surrogates or health care agents. Finally, it would expand to the involuntary euthanasia of incompetent patients whom physicians or others believe no longer have any quality of life. The expansion of patient rights to include the use of advance directives and surrogates for euthanasia might bear some truth, as the use of advance directives and surrogate decision-making which can result in a patient's death is seen to be valid under certain conditions in several countries. In the USA, for example, court rulings from the Quinlan decision to the Cruzan decision have upheld the authority of advance directives and surrogate decision making when patients have made their philosophical intentions known prior to loss of competence. This, indeed, is the basis of living will provisions that presently exist.

In essence, the courts might eventually see no difference between 'allowing to die' and easing suffering by providing for a patient's death more quickly. In terms of moving to non-voluntary euthanasia, opponents of assisted death point to both the Netherlands, and Nazi Germany as examples to be avoided. These arguments, however, ignore the facts. In the Netherlands, qualified patients can request and receive either lethal prescriptions or direct euthanasia (lethal injections). Government studies have found that some 1,000 patients a year meet death in such an involuntary manner. What is lost in this argument is that the Dutch make no distinction between passive and active euthanasia in their statistics, and that many of these 'life terminating acts without explicit request' (LAWER) result from the withholding or withdrawing of life-sustaining treatment – a practice that is widespread in America. In addition, many other such deaths in the Netherlands involved prior discussions between patients and physicians. These LAWER cases have come to public attention only because the Dutch have created a system that allows qualified patients to request and receive assistance, and requires physicians to report them.

Also ignored is the fact that non-voluntary 'euthanasia' is common in American hospitals but goes unreported as these deaths are often sheltered under the wider umbrella of 'double effect'. In many other cases, especially those involving terminal sedation – or what has been termed 'slow euthanasia' – death is the end result of high-dosage sedation together with the withholding of nutrition and hydration. Obviously, death is the intended result of many such actions. In this way the 'slippery slope' already exists. Legalisation of aid in dying can actually provide the controls that can do much to make this slope explicit, and bring existing abuses to light.

In terms of Nazi Germany, what opponents seem to forget is that official programmes for euthanasia were designed from above with the intention, from the very beginning, of gradually creating a system of genocide rooted in the concept of racial purity. This was never voluntary nor based on freedom of choice. The true slippery slope in Nazi Germany was the loss of civil liberty and freedoms. The current call for legalised assisted dying is based on freedom of choice! Restricting freedom of choice and enforcing a public health model which protects individuals from harming themselves – even the terminally ill – is far more dangerous than an approach which provides guarantees of broad freedoms to every individual, including the freedom to choose the time and manner of one's own death.

A rebuttal to the slippery slope argument

From the Voluntary Euthanasia Society of England and Wales.

This argument states that once we have made voluntary euthanasia legal, society will soon allow involuntary euthanasia. This is based on the idea that if we change the law to allow a person to help somebody to die, we will not be able to control it. This is misleading and inaccurate – voluntary euthanasia is based on the right to choose for yourself. It is totally different from murder. There is no evidence to suggest that strictly controlled voluntary euthanasia would inevitably lead to the killing of the sick or elderly against their will. As Ronald Dworkin, Professor of Law at Oxford and New York University, said in 1994:

'Of course doctors know the moral difference between helping people who beg to die and killing those who want to live. If anything, ignoring the pain of terminally-ill patients pleading for death rather than trying to help them seems more likely to chill a doctor's human instincts.'

People who do not agree with voluntary euthanasia often refer to the 1967 Abortion Act. They argue that the numbers of abortions which now take place every year show that the safeguards set out in the Abortion Act have been ignored. They argue that this example should be taken as a warning of what could happen if helping people who are terminally ill to die is made legal. They believe that the law would not be able to control a huge amount of euthanasia cases, many of which would be involuntary. However, abortion is a very different issue to assisted dying. It is also important to remember that people choose to have abortions, they are not forced on people. There is no evidence to suggest that assisted dying will be forced on anyone either.

➪ The above information is reprinted with kind permission from The World Federation of Right to Die Societies. Visit www.worldrtd.net for more information.

© The World Federation of Right to Die Societies

Brief answers to five objections

Information from South Australia Voluntary Euthanasia Society (SAVES).

We cannot always be sure that the patient wants to die

There are no absolute certainties in medical practice but this does not eliminate the need, at times, for doctors to make life and death decisions. Faced with a request for euthanasia, the doctor would follow prescribed guidelines which would include being satisfied that the strength and persistence of the request left no reasonable doubt as to the patient's firm and rational intention.

We cannot always be sure that there is no possibility of cure or return to an acceptable quality of life

Cures take years to discover, test and become generally available. The doctor would discuss the prognosis so that the patient could make an informed decision as to whether a cure or remission was worth waiting for.

Palliative care is now so effective that no-one need ever ask for euthanasia

There are acknowledged limits to palliative care. There are still cases in which pain cannot be satisfactorily controlled, but of greater concern is the loss of faculties and descent into total dependence on others over a lengthy period as a miserable prelude to death. The June 2002 Morgan Poll revealed that only 23% of those polled considered that palliative care was sufficient.

Efforts to find cures and to improve palliative care will be discouraged

The will to live is so strong that no-one wishes to die while their life can still have reasonable quality. There will always be pressure to find cures and improve treatment. Euthanasia would only be an option for those whom current medical skills could not help. The incentive to perfect those skills would remain.

It is always wrong to shorten life deliberately

Those who have this conviction would be free to abstain, either as doctor or patient, but should not deny the option to those who do not share their belief. Most people hold that life should not be taken unlawfully: they accept that there are circumstances in which the taking of life at the request of the patient may be justified and that the law should provide for these.

➪ The above information is reprinted with kind permission from South Australian Voluntary Euthanasia Society (SAVES). Visit www.saves.asn.au for more information.

© South Australian Voluntary Euthanasia Society

ENOUGH!

Need for change

Unbearable suffering, prolonged by medical care and inflicted on a dying patient who wishes to die, is unequivocally a bad thing.

By Raymond Tallis, Emeritus Professor of Geriatric Medicine, University of Manchester

A few years ago, I was chairing a leading medical ethics committee and we had been asked to consider the first Bill put forward by Lord Joffe to legalise assisted dying for people with terminal illness. We opposed the Bill. Some members of the committee did so on religious grounds or on the basis of what they saw as ethical principles. The hostility of the many, including myself, against the assisted dying legislation was based on assumptions we had about its possible longer-term consequences on the practice of medicine and more broadly in society.

The case for a similar Bill to me now seems clear. Unbearable suffering, prolonged by medical care, and inflicted on a dying patient who wishes to die, is unequivocally a bad thing. And respect for individual autonomy – the right to have one's choices supported by others, to determine one's own best interest, when one is of sound mind – is a sovereign principle. Nobody else's personal views should override this.

So where did my initial opposition come from? I was in thrall to numerous incorrect assumptions. But the evidence changed my mind.

Several of my assumptions related to palliative care. Wouldn't assisted dying be unnecessary if the best palliative care were universally available? This is not true and I should have acknowledged this from my experience as a doctor for more than 35 years, when I treated patients whose symptoms were uncontrolled even when they had first-rate palliative care. International experience also confirms that palliative care fails some patients. For the last ten years, assisted suicide has been legal in Oregon under the Death with Dignity Act. Oregon has among the best palliative care of all the states in America and yet nearly 90% of those seeking assisted dying do so from within those services.

I was advised that the availability of assisted dying as an 'easy' option would inhibit investment in palliative care. Again, international experience does not support this. In many countries, the legalisation and regulation of assisted dying has been accompanied by increasing investment in palliative care services. In Oregon the proportion of people dying in hospice care has increased from 37% in 2002 to 52% in 2009 – one of the highest rates in the USA.

I also shared the worry that legalising assisted dying would break down trust between doctor and patient. This is not borne out by the evidence. A survey of nine European countries put levels of trust in the Netherlands at the top. And this is not surprising: in countries with assisted dying, discussion of end-of-life care is open, transparent, honest and mature, not concealed beneath a cloud of ambiguity, as it is in the UK. And the knowledge that your doctor will not abandon the therapeutic alliance with you at your hour of greatest need will foster, not undermine, trust.

I was also concerned that legalising assisted dying would take us to the top of a slippery slope leading to the involuntary euthanasia of people who do not wish to die. In fact, to use the ethicist John Harris's phrase, 'if there is a slippery slope, legislation would apply crampons rather than skis'.

In Oregon, whilst numbers have risen since legalisation, overall numbers have remained low (under 0.2% of all deaths) and the kinds of people being helped to die have not changed. The Dutch experience was to me decisive. Rates of non-voluntary euthanasia (i.e. doctors actively ending patients' lives without having been asked by them to do so) decreased from 0.8% of all deaths in 1990 (approximately 1,000 deaths) to 0.4% in 2005 (approximately 550 deaths).

In the UK, a study published in *Palliative Medicine* found that 0.21% (approximately 1,000) of deaths attended by a medical practitioner in the UK were as a result of voluntary euthanasia. The study also found that 0.3% (approximately 1,500) of life was ended as a result of non-voluntary euthanasia. The present clinical, ethical and legal fudge – in which ploys such as continuous sedation, and starvation and dehydration, are used to get round the prohibition on assisted dying – is unacceptable.

The availability of assisted dying would bring much comfort to many more sufferers than actually use it because it brings a sense of having some control

As a geriatrician, I was also worried that assisted dying would be offered to, or imposed upon, those who are most disempowered. A very detailed analysis of the data in Oregon has shown that there is an under-representation of those groups and an over-representation of comparatively well-off, middle-class white people – feisty characters who are used to getting their own way.

These were the facts that prompted me to change my mind. Even those who accepted these facts still opposed legislation on the grounds that only a small minority of dying people would seek assistance and an even smaller number would use the prescription. Wouldn't legislation prove a sledgehammer to crack a nut?

Well, I happen to believe that even small numbers of people going through unbearable hell are important. The availability of assisted dying would bring much comfort to many more sufferers than actually use it because it brings a sense of having some control.

Death from dehydration and starvation in patients, who have no means of securing an end to their suffering other than by refusing food and fluids, or botched suicides, reflect the unspeakable cruelty of the present law. To accede to someone's request for assisted dying under the circumstances envisaged by Dignity in Dying and others is not to devalue human life, or devalue the life of a particular human being, or to collude in their devaluing their own life. It is to accept their valuation of a few remaining days or weeks of life that they do not wish to endure.

As a result of the courageous action of Debbie Purdy, those who assist their loved ones on grim pilgrimages to Switzerland may be confident that they will not face prosecution. But we have a legal vacuum. Legalisation of physician-assisted dying is needed urgently.

⇨ The above information is reprinted with kind permission from Healthcare Professionals for Assisted Dying (HPAD). Visit www.hpad.org.uk for more information.

© Healthcare Professionals for Assisted Dying

Alternatives to euthanasia and assisted suicide

There are a number of alternative approaches and options for people with terminal conditions or those experiencing intolerable suffering. These are described below.

Refusing treatment

Under English law, all adults have the right to refuse medical treatment, even if that treatment is required to save their life, as long as they have sufficient capacity (the ability to use and understand information to make a decision).

Under the terms of the Mental Capacity Act (2005), all adults are presumed to have sufficient capacity to decide on their own medical treatment, unless there is significant evidence to suggest otherwise.

The evidence has to show that:

⇨ a person's mind or brain is impaired or disturbed;

⇨ the impairment or disturbance means the person is unable to make a decision at the current time.

Examples of impairments or disturbances in the mind or brain include:

⇨ brain damage due to severe head injury, stroke or dementia;

⇨ mental health conditions such as psychosis (where a person is unable to tell the difference between reality and their imagination);

⇨ any physical illness causing delirium.

Under English law, all adults have the right to refuse medical treatment, even if that treatment is required to save their life

If someone makes a decision about treatment that most people would consider to be irrational, it does not constitute a lack of capacity if the person making the decision understands the reality of their situation.

For example, a person may refuse a course of chemotherapy for life-threatening cancer because they would rather not tolerate the side effects of chemotherapy for the sake of a slightly longer life. They understand the reality of their situation and the consequences of their actions and have made a perfectly rational decision.

However, someone with severe (psychotic) depression who refuses treatment because they wrongly believe

there is no hope for recovery and they are so worthless they deserve to die would be considered incapable of making a rational decision. This is because they do not understand the reality of their situation.

Advance decisions

If you know that your capacity to consent may be affected in the future – for example, because you may become unconscious – you can pre-arrange a legally binding advance decision (previously known as an advance directive).

An advance decision sets out the procedures and treatments that you consent to, and the procedures and treatments that you do not consent to. This means that the healthcare professionals treating you cannot perform certain procedures or treatments against your wishes.

For an advance decision to be valid, it must be very specific about what you do not want done and under what circumstances. For example, if you want to refuse a certain treatment, even if it means your life is at risk, you must clearly state this.

The healthcare professionals who are treating you must follow the advance decision, as long as it is valid and applicable: in other words, it covers exactly the condition you go on to develop and the treatment decision now at issue, and there is no doubt about your capacity at the time of drawing up the advance decision. If there is any doubt about the advance decision, the case can be referred to the Court of Protection, which is the legal body that oversees the Mental Capacity Act (2005).

Cardiopulmonary resuscitation and 'Do Not Attempt Resuscitation' orders

Cardiopulmonary resuscitation (CPR) is a treatment that attempts to restore breathing and blood flow in people who have experienced cardiac arrest (when the heart stops beating) or respiratory arrest (when they stop breathing).

CPR is a relatively intensive type of treatment that can involve chest compressions (pressing hard down on the chest), electrical shocks to stimulate the heart, injections of medication and artificial ventilation of the lungs.

Despite the best efforts of medical staff, CPR does not have a good success rate. If CPR is performed in hospital, only one in five people survive. If it is performed outside hospital, only one in ten people survive.

Even when CPR is successful, a person can often develop serious and sometimes painful complications such as:

⇨ fractured ribs;

⇨ damage to the liver and spleen;

⇨ brain damage leading to disability.

Also, many people who do survive then require admission and prolonged treatment in an intensive care unit, where they may die anyway.

Due to the low success rate and the corresponding high risk of complications, many people, especially those with terminal illnesses, make it clear to their medical team that they do not want to be treated with CPR in the event of respiratory or cardiac arrest.

Palliative sedation is not intended to end lives, but the medication carries a risk of shortening life. This has led some critics to argue that palliative sedation is a type of euthanasia

This is known as a 'Do Not Attempt Resuscitation' or DNAR order. Once a DNAR order is made, it is placed with your medical records.

If you have a serious illness or you are undergoing surgery that could cause respiratory or cardiac arrest, a member of your medical team should ask you about your wishes regarding CPR, if you have not previously made your wishes known.

A DNAR choice is not permanent and you can change your DNAR status at any time.

Some supporters of euthanasia have argued that DNAR is essentially a form of passive euthanasia, as a person is being denied treatment that could save their life.

The counter argument to this is that the success rate of CPR is often so low and the risks of complications so high that it is not the case that they are being denied a life-saving treatment. Rather, the risks of CPR far outweigh the benefits, so the treatment should not be used as it will have little to no benefit to the individual concerned.

Palliative sedation

Palliative sedation involves giving a person medication

to make them unconscious and, therefore, unaware of pain. It is often used in people with terminal illnesses.

Many terminal illnesses can cause distressing and painful symptoms when the person reaches their final stages, such as:

⇨ muscle spasms;

⇨ bone pain;

⇨ unpleasant and sometimes frightening breathing difficulties;

⇨ upsetting emotions and feelings such as fear, apprehension and distress.

Palliative sedation is a way of relieving needless suffering.

While palliative sedation is not intended to end lives, the medication carries a risk of shortening life. This has led some critics to argue that palliative sedation is a type of euthanasia.

A counter argument is known as the 'doctrine of double effect'. This states that a treatment that has harmful side effects is still ethical as long as treatment was in the best interests of the patient and the harmful side effects were not intended. For example, very few people would argue that chemotherapy is unethical, even though it can cause a wide range of harmful side effects.

Withdrawing life-sustaining treatments

There are many different treatments that can be used to sustain life in people with serious or terminal illnesses, such as:

⇨ nutritional support through a feeding tube;

⇨ dialysis, where a machine takes over the functions of your kidneys;

⇨ ventilators, where a machine takes over your breathing.

Eventually, there will come a time when it is clear that the prospects of a person recovering are nil and, in the case of terminal illness, the life-sustaining treatments are only prolonging the dying process.

In such circumstances, the doctors would recommend that the person be sedated (if they are not already sedated) and the treatments withdrawn so they can die peacefully in their sleep.

Last reviewed 2 September 2010

⇨ Reproduced by kind permission of the Department of Health. Please visit www.nhs.uk for more information on this and other related topics.

NHS CHOICES

What is the relationship between assisted suicide dying and palliative care?

An extract from Commission on Assisted Dying: Demos Briefing Paper.

What is the purpose of palliative care?

In 2002 the World Health Organization (WHO) defined palliative care as:

'An approach that improves the quality of life of patients and their families facing the problems associated with life-threatening illness, through the prevention and relief of suffering by means of early identification and impeccable assessment and treatment of pain and other problems, physical, psychosocial and spiritual.'

According to the WHO definition, palliative care specifically:

⇨ provides relief from pain and other distressing symptoms;

⇨ affirms life and regards dying as a normal process;

⇨ intends neither to hasten or postpone death;

⇨ integrates the psychological and spiritual aspects of patient care;

⇨ offers a support system to help patients live as actively as possible until death;

⇨ offers a support system to help the family cope during the patient's illness and in their own bereavement;

⇨ uses a team approach to address the needs of patients and their families, including bereavement counselling, if indicated;

⇨ will enhance quality of life, and may also positively influence the course of illness;

⇨ is applicable early in the course of illness, in conjunction with other therapies that are intended to prolong life, such as chemotherapy or radiation therapy, and includes those investigations needed to better understand and manage distressing clinical complications.

In 2004, the House of Commons Health Committee's report on palliative care emphasised the distinction between general and specialist palliative care. General palliative care 'is provided by the usual professional carers of the patient and family, such as GPs, district nurses, hospital doctors, ward nurses, allied health professionals and staff in care homes. Most palliative care is provided by non-specialist staff such as these'.

Specialist palliative care 'is provided by multi-disciplinary teams that might include consultants in palliative medicine, nurse specialists, specialist social workers and experts in psychological care'.

Such staff are specifically trained to advise on symptom control and pain relief and 'to give emotional, psychosocial and spiritual support to patients, their families, friends and carers, both during the patient's illness and into bereavement'.

What is the availability of palliative care in the UK?

According to expert witnesses for the House of Lords Select Committee on the Assisted Dying for the Terminally Ill Bill, palliative care in the UK is 'of a very high quality but inadequately resourced and unevenly spread'.

About 500,000 people die in England each year, with almost two-thirds of people aged over 75. More than half (58 per cent) of deaths take place in NHS hospitals, with about 18 per cent occurring at home, 17 per cent in care homes and three per cent elsewhere. In 2008 there were 175 adult inpatient specialist palliative care units in England, of which 133 were in the voluntary sector and

42 in the NHS. These provide 2,645 specialist palliative care beds, of which 2,141 were in the voluntary sector and 504 in the NHS. In addition to this there were 93 'Hospice at Home' services, 231 Home Care services, 225 Day Care services, 29 Hospital Support Nurses and 226 Hospital Support Teams. As these numbers show, despite recent improvements there continues to be significant under-provision of palliative care services in England.

In 2004, the House of Commons Health Committee on Palliative Care identified inequity of provision as a key issue in the delivery of palliative care. The particular inequities that were identified were:

Inequity by geographical area

The Health Committee found that in many areas there was 'a severe mis-match between service provision and need' and concluded that: 'There is need for more equitable distribution of both hospices and of care at home through an assessment of the needs of the population, greater planning of services and the introduction of detailed contracting arrangements.'

> **There is now a consensus on the issue that high quality palliative care should be made available to all patients at the end of their lives**

Inequity by patient group

Palliative care services for adolescents and young adults were described to the Health Committee as being 'very patchy' and it was felt that they were not sufficiently strategically planned. Age Concern expressed concern that some older patients were less likely to receive referrals to specialist palliative care services than younger patients. There was evidence of inequity by ethnicity, as a number of studies have demonstrated the under-representation of black and minority ethnic communities in palliative care. There was also evidence that patients with complex needs and especially those with learning disabilities may be less able to secure access to palliative care services.

Inequity by disease

The Health Committee commented that 'the lack of palliative care for non-cancer sufferers constituted a major and recurrent theme of our evidence'. The Department of Health agreed that inequity by disease was the most significant inequity in palliative care services. Whereas 95 per cent of those in hospices have cancer, cancer is the cause of death in only a quarter of the population.

The Department of Health's *End of Life Care Strategy*, published in July 2008, acknowledged the continuing under-provision of palliative care services for non-cancer patients and identified 'enhanced specialist palliative care services for people with conditions other than cancer, including additional services in care homes' as a key area that requires greater investment. It found that patients dying from cancer have a much greater likelihood of dying in a hospice than other patients (16 per cent of cancer patients die in a hospice compared with four per cent overall and less than one per cent of patients with circulatory or respiratory disease), despite the fact that those with cancer and those with other diseases tend to experience similar problems in the last year of life.

The report concluded that: 'The challenge for the NHS and social care services now, is to extend this quality of care from the minority of patients (mainly those with cancer) who currently come into contact with hospices and specialist palliative care services, to all people who are approaching the end of life.'

Is palliative care always effective in relieving suffering?

As the above discussion illustrates, there is now a consensus on the issue that high-quality palliative care should be made available to all patients at the end of their lives, regardless of their medical condition, age, ethnicity or location. The House of Lords Select Committee on the Assisted Dying for the Terminally Ill Bill found that there was also general agreement among the witnesses who presented evidence that there are limitations in the degree to which palliative care is able to relieve all dimensions of dying patients' suffering.

The evidence presented to the Select Committee suggested that in most cases, 'good palliative care… can largely relieve the symptoms of physical pain'. However, witnesses including the Voluntary Euthanasia Society and the British Medical Association observed that the psychological suffering that derives from some patients' distress at their irreversible loss of autonomy can be much harder to address than physical symptoms, and that it is this type of suffering that is most likely to give rise to a request for an assisted death.

The Select Committee concluded that: 'The demand for assisted suicide or voluntary euthanasia is particularly strong among determined individuals whose suffering derives more from the fact of their terminal illness than from its symptoms and who are unlikely to be deflected from their wish to end their lives by more or better palliative care. However, opinion continues to be strongly divided on the subject of whether assisted dying could play a complementary role in conjunction with palliative care, or must necessarily conflict with the aims and ethos of palliative care.'

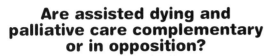

Are assisted dying and palliative care complementary or in opposition?

Generally speaking, people's opinions on the relationship between assisted dying and palliative care tend to correspond with their overall position on the issue of assisted dying. As one study has noted:

'VE/AS legalisation advocates and palliative care providers typically have an adversarial relationship to one another regarding the question of assisted death.'

Those who are against the legalisation of assisted dying tend to argue that assisted dying conflicts with and undermines the principles of palliative care, while those who support the legalisation of assisted dying tend to argue that establishing a legal process to support assisted dying can work alongside and complement palliative care. Some key arguments in support of each position are identified below.

Arguments supporting the perspective that assisted dying and palliative care are in conflict

⇨ There is no type of suffering that cannot be relieved if patients have access to expert palliative care, provided by staff with the right training; therefore, assisted dying is not an appropriate response to suffering.

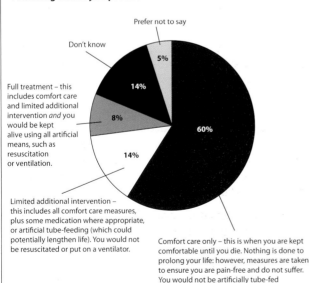

Respondents were asked: 'If you were dying *with no prospect of recovery* – in the last days and weeks of life, which ONE of the following would you prefer?'

Prefer not to say — 5%
Don't know — 14%
Full treatment – this includes comfort care and limited additional intervention *and* you would be kept alive using all artificial means, such as resuscitation or ventilation. — 8%
Limited additional intervention – this includes all comfort care measures, plus some medication where appropriate, or artificial tube-feeding (which could potentially lengthen life). You would not be resuscitated or put on a ventilator. — 14%
Comfort care only – this is when you are kept comfortable until you die. Nothing is done to prolong your life: however, measures are taken to ensure you are pain-free and do not suffer. You would not be artificially tube-fed or resuscitated. — 60%

Base: 2008 adults. Fieldwork: April 2011

Source: YouGov poll on awareness of end-of-life rights, April 2011, Commissioned by Compassion in Dying © YouGov plc. (www.yougov.com)

⇨ Governments should focus on ensuring that their citizens' needs for palliative care services are adequately met before they consider the legalisation of assisted suicide.

⇨ If some form of assisted dying is legalised in order to respond to patients' unbearable suffering, there may be less incentive to improve palliative care and palliative care could be 'underdeveloped' or 'devalued' across the board as a result.

⇨ Palliative care aims to provide people with the best possible quality of life throughout the dying process. Providing assistance for the terminally ill to end their lives prematurely implies the value judgement that dying people's lives are less valuable to our society. This contradicts and undermines the principles underpinning palliative care.

⇨ A patient's request for an assisted death is sometimes in fact a veiled request for reassurance and support in the face of considerable suffering. What the patient may actually be asking for is good palliative care. In these circumstances, an assisted death would not meet the patient's real, underlying needs for support and might increase their feelings of abandonment.

Arguments supporting the perspective that assisted dying and palliative care could be complementary

⇨ While high-quality palliative care will provide an effective solution to suffering towards the end of life for the majority of people, there is a small group of people for whom palliative care is not an effective response to their suffering. Those people for whom palliative care is ineffective and who would rather end their life than continue to experience unbearable suffering, should have the option of an assisted death.

⇨ There would not necessarily be less investment in palliative care if some form of assisted dying was legalised. There might be greater investment in the development of palliative care if the alternative was that patients might want to shorten their lives.

⇨ Both palliative care and assisted dying regimes are driven by values of supporting patients' autonomy and acting with compassion, therefore they are not fundamentally in conflict with one another.

⇨ Trust in doctors could be strengthened.

November 2010

⇨ The above information is an extract from Demos' report *Commission on Assisted Dying: Demos Briefing Paper*, and is reprinted with permission. Visit www.commissiononassisteddying.co.uk for more.

© Demos

DEMOS

End-of-life issues and palliative care

Information from the Scottish Churches Parliamentary Office.

Background

Recent years have seen regular media coverage of individuals who have sought assistance to end their lives. At the centre of these discussions are questions about the value of human life, and the value of autonomy. The secular debate has focused on the right of the individual to choose how they die; this does not lead everyone to support assisted suicide. In fact, medical professionals and disability groups have been strong campaigners against changes to the law because of their concern for the vulnerable and for the effect on the people who would assist in the deaths of others. Religious opponents of assisted suicide have raised varied concerns including the sanctity of life and the need to put the wellbeing of society as a whole above that of the individual. The argument has been that allowing assisted suicide changes for the worse how we, as a society, see the frail and the ill.

Integral to this debate has been the place of palliative care in managing the end of life. Palliative care, sometimes known as symptomatic treatment, aims to relieve suffering and improve quality of life. Palliative care is suitable in many conditions, for example heart failure and dementia, not just for cancer. It is not tied to the end of life, but when death is expected a palliative approach is usually appropriate. It has been argued that greater availability of palliative care would remove, or reduce, the need for assisted suicide.

For people with cancer who die in Scotland, about a half will die in an acute hospital, one-quarter will die at home, and just under one-fifth will die in a hospice. Most palliative care occurs outside of hospices.

Issues

The public debate in Scotland has become increasingly focused on creating legal change rather than more organic social change. In Scottish Parliament an attempt was made to pass legislation legalising assisted suicide by a medical professional. This proposed legislation, the End of Life Assistance (Scotland) Bill, was strongly opposed by many Christians, disability groups and medical professionals. In 2010 the Scottish Parliament rejected the Bill at the first stage of the Parliamentary process with a clear majority.

An attempt has also been made to legislate for the provision of palliative care in the Palliative Care (Scotland) Bill. The Scottish Parliament responded by clearly stating that palliative care provision should not be the subject of legislation, but rather the effectiveness of the *Living and Dying Well* strategy (2008) should be evaluated before further action is taken. Palliative care can be costly. These costs reduce opportunities for the development and delivery of other NHS Scotland services. This raises questions as to how to balance resources devoted to palliative care versus curative treatments.

Questions

⇨ Do you support the principle of assisted dying? If so, what safeguards should be put in place?

⇨ What resources would you like to see devoted to achieving high-quality palliative care, and where would you find the money to do this?

Note

End of life and palliative care issues are matters devolved to the Scottish Parliament under the terms of the Scotland Act 1998, and so law and policy in this area may differ in Scotland to that in England.

10 March 2011

⇨ The above information is reprinted with kind permission from the Scottish Parliament. Visit www.scottish.parliament.uk or www.actsparl.org for more.

© *Scottish Churches Parliamentary Office*

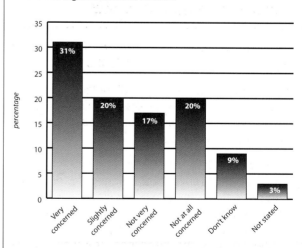

Helping another person to commit suicide is against the law. How concerned or otherwise would you be about a change in the law to legalise assisted suicide?

Category	Percentage
Very concerned	31%
Slightly concerned	20%
Not very concerned	17%
Not at all concerned	20%
Don't know	9%
Not stated	3%

ComRes surveyed 533 disabled people on the Disabled People's Panel between 21 February and 16 March 2011 online. ComRes is a member of the British Polling Council and abides by its rules. Full data tables can be found at www.comres.co.uk

Source: Scope assisted suicide survey, *May 2011* © ComRes.

Poll shows disabled people's fears over assisted suicide

Some 70% of disabled people would be concerned if the law on assisted suicide were to change because they feel it would lead to pressure being placed on disabled people to end their lives.

Findings from a new Scope-commissioned ComRes survey of disabled people also reveals some 56% feel the legalisation of assisted suicide would be detrimental to the way that disabled people are viewed by society as a whole.

The news comes as the BBC announced that it is to screen a documentary where novelist Sir Terry Pratchett, a supporter of euthanasia, follows a man as he travels to Swiss clinic Dignitas to end his life.

Meanwhile, actor Sir Patrick Stewart has thrown his weight behind the Dignity in Dying campaign. On the other side of the debate Care Not Killing has slammed the BBC as a 'cheerleader for assisted suicide'.

Assisted suicide is the act of helping someone else to end their life. It remains illegal in the UK, but in recent years there have been calls to 'clarify' or change the law.

A commission on assisted dying has been set up to gather evidence on the issue – but it is not an official Government commission and there have been questions raised about its impartiality.

Assisted suicide is the act of helping someone else to end their life

At the same time, high-profile members of the legal and medical profession have waded in to the debate.

Scope commissioned the poll of disabled people in a bid to get behind the headlines and make sure disabled people's views and opinions were heard amid the increasingly polarised debate.

Richard Hawkes, Chief Executive of disability charity Scope, said: 'Assisted suicide is a complex and emotional issue, and there are loud and passionate voices on both sides of the debate. But while high-profile lawyers, doctors and celebrities such as Terry Pratchett and Sir Patrick Stewart grab the headlines, the views of the thousands of ordinary disabled people who could be affected by this issue are rarely listened to.

'Our survey findings confirm that concerns about legalising assisted suicide are not just held by a minority,

but by a substantial majority of those this law would affect.

'Disabled people are already worried about people assuming their life isn't worth living or seeing them as a burden, and are genuinely concerned that a change in the law could increase pressure on them to end their life.

'These results should strike a note of caution for all sides, and show how vital a genuinely balanced and open debate on the issue is.

'We have serious concerns about the so-called "Commission" on Assisted Dying, which despite its name is nothing to do with the Government. It feels like their findings are a foregone conclusion, with the debate loaded in favour of assisted suicide. The Government needs to form its own independent non-biased commission to explore this.'

Notes

ComRes surveyed 533 disabled people on the Disabled People's Panel between 21 February and 16 March 2011 online. Data were weighted to be demographically representative of all GB adults. ComRes is a member of the British Polling Council and abides by its rules. Full data tables can be found at www.comres.co.uk

The recent debate started in earnest when, in response to a high-profile legal case, the Law Lords asked the Director of Public Prosecutions (DPP), Keir Starmer, to clarify when someone might be prosecuted when they help someone end their life. The DPP formally issued and published guidelines on 25 February 2010.

Under the current law, assisting someone to commit suicide is punishable by up to 14 years in prison. But, the guidance broadly indicates that family members or friends who help someone to die out of compassion, and not for personal gain or malice, are unlikely to be prosecuted.

9 May 2011

⇨ The above information is reprinted with kind permission from Scope. Visit www.scope.org for more.

Terry Pratchett defends *Choosing to Die documentary from critics*

Critics round on writer and BBC for promoting assisted dying in film that included footage of man's death at Dignitas clinic.

By Haroon Siddique

Sir Terry Pratchett has defended his BBC2 documentary, which showed the death of a millionaire hotelier suffering from motor neurone disease, against criticism from groups opposed to assisted dying.

In *Choosing to Die*, screened on Monday night, the 63-year-old writer, who has Alzheimer's disease, went to the Dignitas clinic in Switzerland to see Peter Smedley take a lethal dose of barbiturates. Michael Nazir-Ali, the retired Bishop of Rochester, condemned the programme as 'science fiction', while Care Not Killing (CNK) described it as 'a recipe for elder abuse and also a threat to vulnerable people'.

Asked why he wanted to make the film, Pratchett told BBC Breakfast: 'Because I was appalled at the current situation. I know that assisted dying is practised in at least three places in Europe and also in the United States. The Government here has always turned its back on it and I was ashamed that British people had to drag themselves to Switzerland, at considerable cost, in order to get the services that they were hoping for.'

Smedley, 71, travelled from his mansion in Guernsey to the clinic, which over the last 12 years has helped 1,100 people to die.

Pratchett said: 'Peter wanted to show the world what was happening and why he was doing it.' He added: 'You can tell in the film that I'm moved. The incongruity of the situation overtakes you. A man has died, that's a bad thing. But he wanted to die, that's a good thing.'

Campaigners accused the BBC of helping to promote assisted dying and of consistently portraying the practice favourably.

Writing on the Christian Concern website, Nazir-Ali said: 'Real life is quite different from Sir Terry's science fiction... The Judaeo-Christian tradition is a surer guide. "Thou shalt not kill" is about acknowledging the gift and dignity of human life which, whether ours or another's, we do not have the competence to take.'

CNK's campaign director, Dr Peter Saunders, said: 'This latest move by the BBC is a disgraceful use of licence-payers' money and further evidence of a blatant campaigning stance. The corporation has now produced five documentaries or docudramas since 2008 portraying assisted suicide in a positive light. Where are the balancing programmes showing the benefits of palliative care, promoting investment on social support for vulnerable people or highlighting the great dangers of legalisation which have convinced parliaments in Australia, France, Canada, Scotland and the US to resist any change in the law in the last 12 months alone?'

Pratchett is a patron of Dignity in Dying, which campaigns for a change in the law to allow assisted dying. The organisation's chief executive, Sarah Wootton, said: 'At the heart of the assisted dying debate, and *Choosing to Die*, is choice and protection. People suffer at the end of life, and therefore people take difficult decisions about their own deaths. As uncomfortable as it may be we need to face up to the reality of what is going on, both at home and abroad.'

14 June 2011

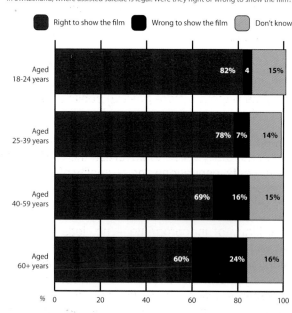

Responses to the following question:

BBC2 will be showing a documentary in which Sir Terry Pratchett, who has been diagnosed with Alzheimer's disease, considers how he might choose to end his life. The documentary contains footage of a man with a terminal disease undergoing an assisted suicide in a clinic in Switzerland, where assisted suicide is legal. Were they right or wrong to show the film?

■ Right to show the film ■ Wrong to show the film ▨ Don't know

	Right to show the film	Wrong to show the film	Don't know
Aged 18-24 years	82%	4	15%
Aged 25-39 years	78%	7%	14%
Aged 40-59 years	69%	16%	15%
Aged 60+ years	60%	24%	16%

Sample size: 2706 GB adults. Fieldwork: 13-14 June 2011.
Source: Dignity in death, June 2011 © YouGov (www.yougov.com)

Whose right is it anyway?

The assisted suicide of a 23-year-old former junior international rugby player rang alarm bells for many disabled people. The subsequent outpourings in our national press have confirmed prejudicial attitudes that demand a response from concerned disabled people, says Paddy Masefield.

Daniel James was not enduring a life-threatening situation. Nor was he burdened with unbearable pain. What he believed he was facing was the 'fear and loathing' of 'a second-class existence' in 'the prison' of his 'crippled' body. These were the words of his mother who had travelled to Switzerland to assist in his suicide a mere 18 months after Daniel broke his neck when a rugby scrum collapsed during training. The words in question were posted on a euthanasia website, an action that resulted in a reader anonymously reporting Mrs James to the police, as assisting suicide is, in the letter of UK law, illegal. Unabashed, Mrs James retorted – 'I hope that one day I (can ask this woman) if she had a son, daughter, father, mother who could not walk… was incontinent and relied upon 24-hour care for every basic need… what would she have done?'

What worries me as much as the disability is the invisibility.

The media in all its forms, from advertising to reality TV shows, has totally failed to advertise the reality of the achievements, aspirations and normality of all disabled people

Of course we all have the right to our private views. It is when they are made public that we also should have a right to reply.

As the majority of all disabled people acquire their impairments in adult life, they will have little notion of their rights without a more positive public presentation of disability.

The media in all its forms, from advertising to reality TV shows, has totally failed to advertise the reality of the achievements, aspirations and normality of all disabled people who merely seek equal rights with their non-disabled fellow citizens.

To the litany of inappropriate – no, let's be honest, downright offensive – language thrown up around Daniel James's change in status, must be added the fearful arguments advanced in the press in support of his family's actions, by philosopher Baroness Mary Warnock, that anyone perceived to be 'completely dependent on others' should automatically have the right to assisted suicide. While journalist Simon Jenkins derided 'one anti-euthanasia lobby (that) even insisted that assisted suicide would deprive the disabled of the benefit of suicide prevention'. Proclaiming that 'to honour this spurious benefit, those wishing to die – and their relatives – must endure unbearable suffering at the bidding of others "for the good of society as a whole".'

I seldom wish ill on others, but I believe Warnock's philosophy might expand, and Jenkins's vocabulary be tutored, were both to experience the meaningful life of many quadriplegics or those with cerebral palsy.

Perhaps the untimely loss of Daniel James should be a positive force for all of us to accept responsibility for ensuring the media tell their stories within a disability context, rather than expecting Disability Now alone to achieve this.

⇨ The above information is reprinted with kind permission from Disability Now. Visit www.disabilitynow.org.uk for more information.

© Disability Now

UK doctors consistently oppose euthanasia and assisted suicide

A review of research carried out over 20 years suggests that UK doctors appear to consistently oppose euthanasia and physician-assisted suicide (PAS). The findings – which appear in the latest issue of the journal Palliative Medicine, *published by SAGE – highlight a gap between doctors' attitudes and those of the UK public.*

The study, carried out by Dr Ruaidhrí McCormack and colleagues Dr M Clifford and Dr M Conroy at the Department of Palliative Medicine, Milford Care Centre, Limerick, Eire, searched through literature from 1990 to 2010 and found 16 key studies. These examined UK doctors' attitudes to either assisted voluntary euthanasia (AVE), or PAS, or both. Qualitative and quantitative data were included.

Definitions of these terms are considered controversial. The authors were guided by the European Association for Palliative Care (EAPC) ethics task force, who defined euthanasia as: 'a doctor intentionally killing a person by the administration of drugs, at that person's voluntary and competent request'. PAS was further defined as: 'a doctor intentionally helping a person to commit suicide by providing drugs for self-administration, at that person's voluntary and competent request'. In both instances, the patient plays an active role and must provide explicit consent.

The majority of doctors opposed AVE in all of the studies but one (11 of the studies examined attitudes to AVE). The majority of doctors were against PAS in eight of the ten studies examining this topic. One study was unclear due to the question phrasing, while a study of ICU physicians demonstrated majority support for PAS. Six studies asked doctors if they would perform these practices were they made legal, on average only about a quarter would be willing (PAS: 25 per cent, AVE: 23 per cent).

One of the strongest predictors of a doctor's unwillingness was religiosity, with the most faithful least likely to consider assisting death, or supporting its UK introduction. Other factors consistently highlighted were that palliative care reduces suffering and limits the need for assisted dying, the need for adequate safeguards were AVE or PAS introduced, and the idea of a profession to facilitate these practices that does not include doctors.

'Further studies are necessary to establish if subgroup variables other than degree of religiosity influence attitudes, and to thoroughly explore the qualitative themes that appeared,' said McCormack. Themes such as AVE/PAS in the contexts of technological advancement, increased 'medicalisation' and reducing futile medical treatment, an opt-out clause for individual doctors, and concern about patient's mental state and level of autonomy all merit future research.

The study was the first systematic review specifically looking at the attitudes of UK doctors. According to a British Social Attitudes survey published in 2007, up to 80 per cent of the British public support voluntary euthanasia by a doctor in the case of terminal illness, and up to 60 per cent support PAS given the same scenario.

9 March 2011

⇨ The above information was accessed through Science Daily, adapted from the original publication in *Palliative Medicine*, published by SAGE Publications. Visit www.sciencedaily.com and www.sagepub.com for more information.

Support grows for 'right to die'

Summary of a study carried out by YouGov.

By Steven McCord

Most British people support the legalisation of assisted suicide where the terminally ill person is able to make the decision themselves, a survey has found. In light of recent media coverage surrounding the right-to-die campaigner Debbie Purdy, 56% of the 3,874 people asked indicated that they felt that assisted suicide was acceptable if the demand to die came solely from the terminally-ill patient.

An overwhelming 88% of people in total would support the legalisation of euthanasia in some form. In addition to those who felt that the terminally ill person should alone be able to make the decision to end their life, 18% went further and said they felt that very close family members should be able to make the decision out of compassion, while 14% indicated that they would support the legalisation of assisted suicide in exceptional circumstances. In contrast, only 7% of those surveyed indicated a full objection to legalising assisted suicide. This may perhaps be because a large proportion of the public still hold fears over retrospective prosecution.

'Mitigating factors'

When questioned about their thoughts on Keir Starmer, the Director of Public Prosecutions', recent introduction of 'mitigating factors' for judicial consideration – which state that in order to escape criminal prosecution, the person assisting suicide should be motivated by compassion, should have attempted to dissuade the patient, be assured of the patient's personal and voluntary determination to die, offer only minor help, and report the suicide to the police – 38% indicated that these proposals don't go far enough, because, as Starmer himself admitted, they do not pre-empt the possible prosecution of someone assisting in a suicide.

36% of those asked described Starmer's proposals as 'sensible', feeling that they covered the issues well. Only 10% characterised the proposals as a 'worrying' step towards the legalisation of euthanasia.

Lack of clarity

While the subject of euthanasia is bedevilled by a lack of definitional clarity, these results suggest that there is considerable support for the qualified legalisation of assisted suicide, even if there is a certain lack of consensus as to what form it should take, and how far it should reach.

8 March 2010

⇨ The above information is reprinted with kind permission from YouGov. Visit http://today.yougov.co.uk for more information.

Assisted dying and the status quo

An extract from Commission on Assisted Dying: Demos Briefing Paper.

The current legal status of assisted suicide in UK law

Deliberately and directly taking the life of another person, whether that person is dying or not, constitutes the crime of murder. The Suicide Act 1961, updated by the Coroners and Justice Act 2009, makes encouraging or assisting a suicide a crime punishable by up to 14 years' imprisonment. The Suicide Act gives the Director of Public Prosecutions (DPP) discretion over whether to prosecute cases of assisting or encouraging suicide – a decision is taken as to whether prosecution is in the public interest.

There have been a number of important cases challenging this law. In 2002, Diane Pretty, who was diagnosed with motor neurone disease, wanted her husband to assist her in committing suicide when she was no longer physically able to do so herself. She asked the DPP to grant him immunity from prosecution. The DPP refused and she subsequently took the request to court. Two UK courts refused the request and the case went to the European Court of Human Rights, but again her request was refused based on the judgement that: 'though she has a right to life, she had no right to death'. The European Court of Human Rights held that 'the notion of personal autonomy is an important principle underlying the interpretation' of the right to respect for private and family life found in Article 8 (1) of the European Convention on Human Rights. However, the court went on to find that any interference with Mrs Pretty's right was compatible with the saving provision in Article 8 (2) as it was necessary 'in pursuit of the legitimate aim of safeguarding life and thereby protecting the rights of others'.

More recently a similar but successful challenge was made to the DPP. In 2009, Debbie Purdy, a woman with primary progressive multiple sclerosis, wanted to know if her husband would be prosecuted if he helped her commit suicide overseas. Her landmark case challenged the law, arguing that the DPP was infringing her human rights by failing to clarify how the Suicide Act is actually enforced. The House of Lords (at the time the highest court; since replaced by the Supreme Court) ruled that

clarification should be given and the DPP was asked to prepare an offence-specific policy to identify the facts and circumstances that he would take into account in deciding, in such cases, whether or not to prosecute.

The Crown Prosecution Service (CPS) subsequently published a Policy for *Prosecutors in Respect of Cases of Encouraging or Assisting Suicide*, that set out 16 public interest factors in favour of prosecution and six against. The policy gives individuals an indication of how they are likely to be treated by police or prosecutors and for the first time gives formal recognition that in some circumstances, people should not be prosecuted for helping someone to die, making a distinction between compassionate and malicious acts of assistance.

To what extent are assisted suicide and euthanasia already happening in the UK?

It was previously thought that covert voluntary euthanasia was a fairly widespread practice amongst the medical profession. A number of surveys were understood to demonstrate this. One survey of GPs and consultants found that 12 per cent of respondents claimed to have complied with a request to prematurely end a patient's life. Another study found that one in seven GPs admitted to helping patients to die and that 'hundreds, probably thousands, of patients die each year with the help of doctors'. A Medix survey in the UK in 2004 found that 45 per cent of doctors understood that their colleagues actively helped their patients die.

However, more recent evidence suggests that the practice of physician-assisted dying is actually much less prevalent than previously thought. In 2004, a survey of end-of-life decisions (ELDs) in the UK, which asked doctors about the most recent death they had attended, found relatively low rates of voluntary and non-voluntary euthanasia and no instances of assisted suicide. These results contrasted with similar versions of the survey conducted in the Netherlands, Belgium and Australia where both euthanasia and assisted suicide were found to be more common. A subsequent

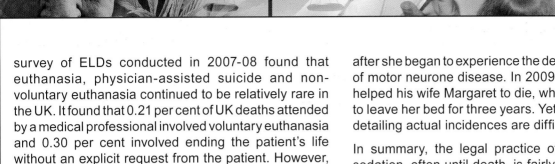

survey of ELDs conducted in 2007-08 found that euthanasia, physician-assisted suicide and non-voluntary euthanasia continued to be relatively rare in the UK. It found that 0.21 per cent of UK deaths attended by a medical professional involved voluntary euthanasia and 0.30 per cent involved ending the patient's life without an explicit request from the patient. However, there were no cases of physician-assisted suicide in the UK according to this survey. This research found that even where decisions are taken with the understanding that they may accelerate death in around a third of cases, they are not regarded as actually affecting the length of a patient's life. The study concluded that the shortening of life by a significant amount is rare in UK medical practice.

Research also by Clive Seale indicates that the use of continuous deep sedation (CDS), which is a palliative practice of relieving pain or distress in the last hours or days of a terminally ill person's life, usually by means of administration of sedative drug, is relatively common. A survey of over 8,000 doctors found that just over 18 per cent of the doctors attending a dying patient reported the use of CDS.

For terminally ill people who wish to die, the right to refuse life-prolonging treatment (including nourishment and hydration) is also firmly established in law. If a patient chose to shorten their life by refusing treatment, this would not be considered an assisted death. Clive Seale's survey of ELDs conducted in 2007-08 found that 21.8 per cent of UK deaths attended by a medical professional involved the withdrawing or withholding of treatment. In the case of Airedale NHS Trust v. Bland in 1993, the House of Lords also confirmed the principle that doctors could withhold life-prolonging treatment from 'an insensate patient in a persistent vegetative state', if that patient's death would follow 'imminently' after the withdrawal of treatment. However, in its ruling the court advised that if similar situations arose in the future, families and doctors should seek advice from the court before taking action, as the right course of action would need to be decided on a case-by-case basis. The court specifically distinguished the action of withholding life-prolonging treatment from euthanasia, which is a criminal offence.

Are assisted suicide and voluntary euthanasia happening outside the confines of the medical profession? At least 150 UK citizens are known to have ended their lives at the Dignitas clinic in Switzerland, with up to 800 more believed to be members, the ethics of which will be discussed in the next section. Home Office statistics report that a very small number of mercy killings (around four) are identified each year. There are occasional high-profile cases of suicides occurring behind closed doors and of amateur assistance with suicide. Recent examples include Michelle Broad, who took her own life

after she began to experience the degenerative impacts of motor neurone disease. In 2009, Michael Bateman helped his wife Margaret to die, who had been unable to leave her bed for three years. Yet accurate statistics detailing actual incidences are difficult to come by.

In summary, the legal practice of continuous deep sedation, often until death, is fairly common and may occur in almost one in five deaths. Equally, there is evidence that the practice of withdrawing or withholding treatment occurs in approximately one in five deaths. However, the most recent evidence available suggests that in the UK, cases of voluntary and non-voluntary euthanasia are relatively rare, with about two in every 1,000 deaths involving voluntary euthanasia and about three in every 1,000 deaths involving non-voluntary euthanasia. No cases of physician-assisted suicide were identified by this research. In addition to these practices, a small number of individuals are known to travel from the UK each year to end their lives in Switzerland, and a similarly small number of cases on mercy killing and amateur assistance with suicide are also believed to take place.

Advantages and disadvantages of the current legal position on assisted dying

The current legal situation under the new CPS policy has been criticised for being discriminatory. Jonathan Glover from the Centre of Medical Law and Ethics, King's College London, has argued that it is 'discriminatory

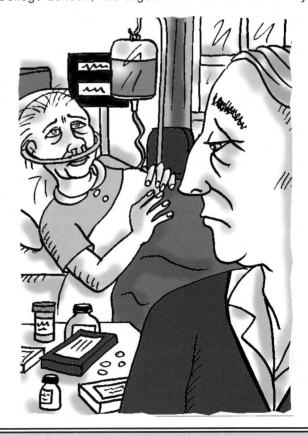

and objectionable that somebody who is capable of committing suicide is able to do that, but somebody who happens to lack the physical capacity to do that is denied it'. Questions of equality also surround the practice of attending Dignitas for the purposes of 'suicide tourism'. Above and beyond issues surrounding the operating principles of Dignitas, this poses a serious issue of equality: is it right that those who can afford to travel to Switzerland are able to end their life whilst those who do not have the financial capability cannot and might attempt to do so at home, in secret?

What are the implications of the DPP policy?

The DPP *Policy for Prosecutors in Respect of Cases of Encouraging or Assisting Suicide* was welcomed by many individuals and organisations as an important source of clarification of the law with regards to assisted suicide. Care not Killing welcomed the fact that 'the law has not changed, that no-one has immunity from prosecution, and that a prosecution will normally follow unless there are clear and compelling public interest factors to the contrary'. Care not Killing and SPUC Pro-Life also both welcomed the fact that the characteristics of terminal illness or disability in the assisted person were not identified as factors tending against prosecution, which they argued would mean providing people who have disabilities or who are ill with less legal protection than other groups.

However, some critics have argued that the previous unofficial policy of non-prosecution in cases of 'assisted suicide-tourism' that existed before the DPP policy was preferable, as this did not risk normalising or condoning assisted suicide. Other critics have argued that while the DPP policy 'does not change the law on assisted suicide' and 'does not open the door for euthanasia' the policy could be construed as 'seeking to change the law by the back door', and the 'checklist approach could legalise killing because it becomes far easier for people to hide the fact if they are acting out of bad motives'. Furthermore, others argue that whilst the policy does provide some much needed clarity over the law, the policy still cannot provide a safeguarded means for assisted dying; and that the policy condones terminally ill people travelling abroad to die but does not allow them the choice to die at home at a time of their choosing.

Penney Lewis, Professor of Law at King's College London, has also criticised this element of the policy: 'by strongly discouraging medical involvement, the guidelines place a heavy burden on supportive friends and family' with the burden of assistance likely to fall on someone with no experience or access to relevant information. In her response to the CPS consultation on the policy, Professor Penney Lewis noted how a number of the prosecution factors seem concerned with ensuring that assistance remains an amateur

activity carried out by inexperienced individuals without the assistance of either medical professionals or non-medical organisations (such as Dignitas in Switzerland).

Dignity in Dying (DID) also criticised the policy on a number of issues, noting in particular that the policy has shifted emphasis from the characteristics of the assisted person to the motivations of the person that assists. This means that there are no safeguards to determine who should and should not be able to receive assistance which means that there is less protection than would be offered by a change in the law. The policy is unclear about the extent of restrictions on doctors' actions and on what grounds they might be prosecuted for providing assistance. DID argue that this could not only affect doctors' willingness to provide patients with medical records should they want to go abroad, but also to engage in discussion with patients who express a desire to end their life. This could damage the patient's trust of their doctor and patients may turn instead to the Internet for information if their doctor is unwilling to provide it. DID voice concerns that, as a result, assistance with suicide will remain an amateur activity conducted by inexperienced people, with the potential to expose those individuals being assisted to even greater suffering if their suicide attempt goes wrong. DID also argue that the policy's provision of retrospective checks does not protect the public, as up-front safeguards are still lacking.

> ### *The policy condones terminally ill people travelling abroad to die but does not allow them the choice to die at home at a time of their choosing*

The Medical Protection Society have voiced the concern that whilst the DPP policy may bring comfort to individuals and their loved ones facing these difficult issues, the policy 'sends a clear signal that prosecutions are more likely to be brought against healthcare professionals who may be faced with requests from patients regarding assisted suicide'. Also reacting to the policy, the British Medical Association asserted their continued advice for doctors to avoid 'actions that might be interpreted as assisting, facilitating or encouraging a suicide attempt' and stated that they remain opposed to doctors taking a role in any form of assisted dying.

November 2010

⇨ The above information is an extract from Demos' report *Commission on Assisted Dying: Demos Briefing Paper*, and is reprinted with permission. Visit www.demos.co.uk for more information.

© Demos

DEMOS

Legislation is not the answer for assisted suicide

You can't legislate for assisted suicide or euthanasia satisfactorily enough for murder not to go unpunished.

The Government won't consider bringing forward legislation to make assisted suicide legal. This isn't because of morality, religion or even because of a lack of compassion for the terminally ill. The reason is simple: you can't legislate for assisted suicide or euthanasia satisfactorily enough for murder not to go unpunished.

Those who support the idea of legislating in favour of assisted suicide will always give you the philosophical argument that it is our choice when to end our own lives and it should be a choice to be able to die with dignity.

They also tend to trash the religious argument that life is a precious gift from God.

I have no real problem with either of these arguments, but they do not take into account reality. And that is where the law steps in.

The existing law on assisting someone to kill themselves is described in the Suicide Act 1961 as 'a person who aids, abets, counsels or procures the suicide of another, or attempt by another to commit suicide'. It makes the offence punishable by up to 14 years in prison.

But, just as in the case of murder, motive is everything.

The question of why a person helped another end their own life is crucial in the case of assisted suicide, just as the reason why one person killed another is crucial to any murder case.

There is no admission by the Government today or by policymakers in general that assisted suicide is socially and morally acceptable, largely because to an awful lot of people it simply isn't.

What we have been given today is clarity from the Director of Public Prosecutions (DPP) that certain considerations may mean prosecution 'is not in the public interest'. That is the job of the DPP. In fact the sole reason for having a DPP is to give guidance as to when certain prosecutions may or may not be in the public interest.

Take two different examples we have had recently in which two mothers were tried for ending the lives of their children.

Francis Inglis wasn't found guilty of assisting in her son's suicide. She was found guilty of the more serious offence of murder. The reasons for this were several.

Her son was not terminally ill, despite suffering horrific injuries that left him brain damaged. He had not discussed with her what his wishes were in the event that his quality of life was so poor he would rather be dead. She had essentially decided for him. When she administered the lethal dose of heroin that killed him she had already been charged with attempted murder. She also tricked hospital staff into thinking she was someone else.

That she committed murder as an act of compassion was neither here nor there. It was a tragic situation and one can only feel sympathy for her but, act of compassion or not, she made the decision for her son and she was fully aware of what she was doing.

Compare that to the case of Kay Gilderdale, who was found not guilty of murder for helping her daughter to commit suicide.

In this case Mrs Gilderdale had discussed what to do with her daughter before acting. Her daughter had suffered from ME for 17 years. She was paralysed from the waist down, unable to speak, eat or drink and was fed through a tube.

She communicated with her parents through a form of sign language they devised themselves. She had also developed suicidal thoughts, which she published on an online forum.

And she had left a living will as well as a 'do not resuscitate' note on her medical records and considered ending her life at Dignitas, the Swiss-based assisted suicide clinic.

These two cases are fundamentally different and in both the juries should and can be rightly pleased that justice was done. There is no postcode lottery of justice, as some in the media tried to suggest at the time. The cases were utterly different and that's why the laws we have in this area work so well. The only change now is that under this new guidance Mrs Gilderdale may have been spared the additional pain of being tried for murder.

On a slightly more grotesque level, policymakers have to consider that the relatives of a rich aunt might decide to hasten her exit from this life in order to collect their inheritance.

While this might be an unsavoury thought it is one of the fundamental reasons why changing the law on assisted suicide is impractical. Murder could effectively be hidden as assisted suicide.

And which is the more morally repugnant? That people suffer degenerative diseases and die with less dignity than they might have wanted, or that murderers are able to get away with it because they manipulate the law created to allow people to die with that level of dignity that we'd all like?

Of course, what the case of Debbie Purdy and the subsequent guidance from the DPP has provided us with is a third way. Essentially it creates circumstances in which the Crown Prosecution Service can state that prosecution of a certain individual for assisting the suicide of another 'is not in the public interest'. That doesn't make it legal but it does mean accompanying loved ones to Switzerland in order to be with them when they commit suicide is less likely to end in a prison sentence for those left behind.

As always with this subject, emotions will run high and I'm entirely sympathetic to the arguments put forward by those who say that they want the right to die with dignity. I watched my mother die from cancer three years ago and had often had philosophical discussions with her prior to her becoming ill about how she would rather die than become so ill that her family had to care for her.

In some ways my family was fortunate that my mother's illness did not drag on. This might sound heartless but it's not meant to be. I'm simply grateful she didn't suffer. If I'm totally honest I'm also grateful I didn't have to watch her suffer for too long before she died because, as much as I tried to stay positive and lighthearted, every weekend that I spent with her in her final six months broke my heart. Watching my father suffering in his own quiet, dignified way will remain with me for the rest of my life.

And if she had asked me to help her end her life I would like to think I wouldn't have hesitated to help her. The problem is I simply do not know if I would have been brave enough to.

I'd like to think I would. And I think anyone that does is committing a very courageous final act of love.

But doing any more than has been done today by the DPP, creating a law that makes assisted suicide legal, is utterly impossible.

25 February 2010

⇨ The above information is reprinted with kind permission from Politics.co.uk. Visit www.politics.co.uk for more information.

Jurisdictions in which some form of assisted dying is legal

Jurisdiction	Legislation permits	Law
Switzerland	Assisted suicide (non-medical)	Swiss Penal Code (1942)
Oregon	Physician-assisted suicide	Oregon Death with Dignity Act (1994)
The Netherlands	Voluntary euthanasia and physician-assisted suicide	The Termination of Life on Request and Assisted Suicide (Review Procedures Act 2001)
Belgium	Voluntary euthanasia	Law on Euthanasia (2002)
Luxembourg	Physician-assisted suicide and voluntary euthanasia	Law on Euthanasia and Assisted Suicide (2008)
Washington State	Physician-assisted suicide	Washington Death with Dignity Act (2008)
Montana	Physician-assisted suicide	No act*

*No act, but the Supreme Court ruled that: 'nothing in Montana Supreme Court precedent or Montana statutes indicating that physician aid in dying is against public policy'.

Source: Commission on Assisted Dying: Demos Briefing Paper, *November 2010 © Demos.*

We need an assisted dying law

Legal clarification on the consequences of euthanasia is not enough – a statute would give terminally ill people a choice.

By Margaret Jay

I welcome the final decision of the Director of Public Prosecutions, which goes some way to clarifying the law on assisted suicide. As the interim version Keir Starmer published last autumn indicated, the new guidelines will allow people who are considering an assisted death to make better-informed decisions about the likely consequences of their actions to their loved ones. While the DPP has made clear that his new guidelines do not alter the existing law, the six factors that could mitigate against a prosecution emphasise that the Crown Prosecution Service observes a clear distinction between an act of compassionate help towards someone who wants to die and those acts that have a malicious or selfish motivation.

But, however welcome today's guidelines, they will not solve all of the problems that we as a society face around end-of-life decision making. I disagree with Gordon Brown's comments yesterday – ultimately Parliament needs to take responsibility for updating the law. There are two key questions for any proposed legislation: will an assisted dying law with up-front safeguards better protect people against potential abuse, and how should the law deal with those who go beyond assisting, and directly end a loved one's life for compassionate reasons?

These are not theoretical problems. In the last few weeks we've seen some high-profile cases: Kay Gilderdale, Frances Inglis and Ray Gosling. These are often reported as though they are identical and should be considered in identical ethical and legal terms. But, in fact, the three very difficult human stories reflect the extraordinary complexity of different end-of-life decisions which may all be taken on compassionate grounds but will not necessarily be helped by the DPP's new guidelines.

Last month the courts heard the case of Gilderdale. She assisted her chronically ill adult daughter to die by providing her with an overdose of morphine, to inject herself. Due to questions over the extent to which Gilderdale helped her daughter, she was tried for attempted murder as well as assisted suicide, but treated leniently.

In a different courtroom a week before, Inglis was found guilty of murder, an offence which carries a mandatory life sentence. She had given her severely brain-damaged son an injection of heroin in order to end what she imagined for him would be a 'living hell'. The key difference between these two cases was the consent of the person who died and the level of assistance given to help the person die, one case was considered help, the other direct action. As a result of these differences Inglis faces a minimum of nine years in prison, whiles Gilderdale was given a 12-month non-custodial sentence.

Regardless of the factors set out in the DPP's guidance, Inglis would still face life in prison. There is clearly an ethical difference between assisted suicide and involuntary euthanasia and this has to be reflected in sentencing. However, the imposition of a mandatory life sentence for murder can sometimes seem unduly harsh in cases such as Inglis'.

Gosling's case is also considered to be a potential mercy killing as he took the final decision to end his lover's life, even though Gosling says his lover asked him to do this. This means that if there is sufficient evidence to charge Gosling he faces a similar fate to that of Inglis. How do we find a way out of this ethical mess?

In my view, an assisted dying law for those who are terminally ill and mentally competent with up-front safeguards would better protect all people. It would mean considering cases of assisted dying in advance and would highlight any potential abuse before the death. At the moment a post-facto investigation can only discover any evidence of abuse after the person has died. An assisted dying statute would give terminally ill people who are suffering unbearably, and their loved ones, the option of choice and control.

We also need an urgent review of murder law. In 2006, the Law Commission recommended separate categories of offence to cover mercy killing, or a partial defence to cover compassionate cases. The new House of Commons should consider this whole area again. Obviously people who break the law should be investigated, but those who do so out of love and compassion should be treated proportionately and in the context of the motivation for the actions they took.

The DPP's guidelines address one part of the problem, but now we need to address the bigger picture, which is not the application of the law – it's the law itself. Society has moved on; so should Parliament.

25 February 2010

THE GUARDIAN

Scottish Parliament rejects Bill to legalise euthanasia

The Scottish Parliament voted on 1 December 2010 to throw out the End of Life Assistance (Scotland) Bill which proposed to legalise assisted suicide and euthanasia in Scotland.

Margo MacDonald MSP introduced the Bill in February after having conducted an extensive publicity drive in support of her proposal. This included a *Panorama* episode on the issue and a 'fact-finding' trip to Dignitas in Zurich.

The Scottish Parliament overwhelmingly rejected the Bill by 85 votes to 16 with two abstentions. Last month the Committee which looked at the Bill also rejected it by five votes to one. The Committee described the Bill as having an 'extraordinarily wide' scope.

The Bill would have allowed tens of thousands of Scots to gain assistance to end their lives, either through assisted suicide or by active euthanasia. It applied to people with terminal illnesses and also to those who were incapacitated to such an extent as not to be able to live life independently and who found life to be 'intolerable'. Such a loose definition was particularly problematic.

> ### The Scottish Parliament overwhelmingly rejected the Bill by 85 votes to 16 with two abstentions

The Bill contained no conscience clause to protect health professionals, applied to people aged over 16 and required that the end of life assistance was given within 30 days of completion of the application process. This led to fears of a conveyor belt process. There were real concerns over the inadequacy of the 'so-called' safeguards and fears that many vulnerable people would feel pressurised into ending their lives prematurely in order not to be a burden to family or friends.

Nola Leach, Chief Executive of CARE, said:

'We are delighted that the Scottish Parliament has rejected this Bill. The Bill posed real dangers to the sick and vulnerable. Euthanasia and assisted suicide should never be acceptable in a civilised society. Rather there needs to be much more investment in hospice and other palliative care.'

Bill Baird, Manager of CARE for Scotland, said:

'CARE supporters in Scotland have been very active in contacting their MSPs regarding this Bill. Our campaigning has helped convince MSPs to oppose the Bill, because they could see its dangers. Working with our partners in the Care Not Killing alliance we have run a very effective postcard campaign with over 20,000 people expressing to MSPs their opposition to the Bill.'

1 December 2010

⇨ The above information is reprinted with kind permission from CARE (Christian Action Research and Education). Visit www.care.org.uk for more information.

CARE

Impact on the medical profession and doctor–patient relationships

An extract from Potential risks associated with a change in the law from Demos' report Commission on Assisted Dying: Demos Briefing Paper.

The doctor–patient relationship is one founded primarily on trust and opponents to a change in the law argue that by taking on the additional role of assisted dying, trust could be lost and the doctor–patient relationship damaged. The majority of medical practitioners in the UK currently oppose the legalisation of assisted dying and the British Medical Association remains 'opposed to doctors taking a role in any form of assisted dying'. In this regard, it is important that doctors with a conscientious objection to assisted dying should be exempt from taking part.

In what ways might the legalisation of some form of assisted dying affect the integrity of the medical profession? One issue is the practicality of enacting the law if a majority of doctors conscientiously object to assisting their patients to die. The Association for Palliative Medicine, for example, have voiced concerns that legislation could cause a polarisation in the medical profession and lead to the development of a specialist assisted dying sector made up of practitioners who have no interest in offering alternatives to death. There is also the possibility that patients may lose trust in their doctors if they know that assisted death is a 'treatment' option: one survey found that 60 per cent of respondents felt that elderly people might be more nervous of going into hospital if euthanasia were to be legalised.

However, evidence from other countries has as yet shown little or no evidence of these negative impacts. A survey of 11 European countries (including the UK) found that the Dutch had the highest regard and trust for their doctors. Another study looking at end-of-life decisions in six countries in Europe found that the best communication between doctors and their patients and families occurred in the Netherlands.

The majority of medical practitioners in the UK currently oppose the legalisation of assisted dying

This evidence suggests that levels of trust depend on openness and communication between doctors and patients and that for many people, knowing that a doctor is able and willing to end their life if it is in their best interests would promote trust, not reduce it. Respect for patient autonomy is one of most important parts of the doctor–patient relationship and being able to openly discuss all a patient's wishes is central to this. A study by Back *et al* found that the best outcome for patients and their families is when the doctor is able to discuss all of the patient's concerns and requests, including any request for help to die. If the doctor cannot be open to such a discussion, the patient can feel abandoned and suffer further distress.

Research in Oregon and the Netherlands has shown that where some form of assisted dying is permitted, society remains supportive of the legislation. A survey conducted in Oregon in 2004 found that 74 per cent of respondents had become more supportive since the legislation took effect. A survey in the Netherlands in 2001 found that 81 per cent of respondents supported assisted dying.

November 2010

⇨ The above information is an extract from Demos' report *Commission on Assisted Dying: Demos Briefing Paper*, and is reprinted with permission. Visit www. demos.co.uk for more information.

© Demos

Belgian patients are being killed without their consent

Terminally-ill patients in Belgium are being subjected to euthanasia without their consent, according to a shocking study.

The findings are likely to inflame concern that any move to legalise assisted suicide or euthanasia in the UK would leave vulnerable people dangerously exposed.

The study, published in the *Canadian Medical Association Journal (CMAJ)*, suggests that almost half of Belgium's euthanasia deaths may be carried out on patients who have not asked for their lives to be ended.

Euthanasia

It revealed that 248 nurses, representing almost a fifth of the nurses interviewed, had cared for euthanasia patients.

And nearly 50 per cent of these, some 120 nurses, had been involved in killing patients without their 'explicit request'.

Dr Peter Saunders, Director of the pro-life group Care Not Killing, cautioned: 'We should take a warning from this that wherever you draw the line, people will go up to it and beyond it'.

Involuntary

He added: 'Once you have legalised voluntary euthanasia, involuntary euthanasia will inevitably follow'.

Euthanasia has been legal in Belgium since 2002, but the law requires patients to give their consent and states that the death must be facilitated by a doctor.

The report, entitled *The Role of Nurses in Physician Assisted Deaths* in Belgium, supports Dr Saunders' warning.

Without

The report states: 'By administering the life-ending drugs in some of the cases of euthanasia, and in almost half of the cases without an explicit request from the patient, the nurses in our study operated beyond the legal margins of their profession.'

Press reports indicate that euthanasia now accounts for two per cent of Belgium's deaths, the equivalent of around 2,000 people a year.

Harvesting

Last month a bio-ethicist warned that allowing organs to be harvested from euthanasia victims was setting a dangerous precedent.

Wesley Smith's comments followed an article in the bioethics journal *Transplantation* about the euthanasia of a completely paralysed Belgian woman.

The woman, who was killed by intravenous injection, was taken to have her organs removed just ten minutes after her heart activity stopped.

Alarm

Mr Smith, a Senior Fellow at the Discovery Institute in Washington, said: 'If this doesn't set off alarm bells about how the sick and disabled are increasingly being looked upon not only as burdens (to themselves, families and society), but potential objects for exploitation, what will?

The study, published in the Canadian Medical Association Journal (CMAJ), suggests that almost half of Belgium's euthanasia deaths may be carried out on patients who have not asked for their lives to be ended

'A disabled woman was killed, even though people with locked-in states often adjust over time to their disabilities and are happy to be alive.'

He added: 'This case of two separate requests, first euthanasia and second, organ donation after death, demonstrates that organ harvesting after euthanasia may be considered and accepted from ethical, legal and practical viewpoints in countries where euthanasia is legally accepted.'

10 June 2010

⇨ The above information is reprinted with kind permission from The Christian Institute. Visit www. christian.org.uk for more information.

Fearful elderly people carry 'anti-euthanasia cards'

Elderly people in the Netherlands are so fearful of being killed by doctors that they carry cards saying they do not want euthanasia, according to a campaigner who says allowing assistant suicide in Britain would put the vulnerable at risk.

By Martin Beckford, Health Correspondent

Kevin Fitzpatrick, a researcher with the pressure group Not Dead Yet, claimed that relaxing the law in this country would threaten old and disabled people as it would allow 'moral judgements' that their lives were not worth living.

He said it is 'nonsensical' to say that we all have a right to die, when what is really being suggested is the right to a premature death that is not sought by all in society.

Charities and groups supporting disabled people and the elderly fear that any change in the law would leave them feeling under pressure to end their lives

But a former professor of geriatric medicine, Raymond Tallis, also writing online in the *BMJ*, argues that countries which have legalised assisted dying have neither seen trust in medics eroded nor the procedure imposed on vulnerable people.

The debate comes amid an increasingly high-profile campaign in Britain to decriminalise assisted suicide. A court victory last year forced the Director of Public Prosecutions to admit that individuals would not be prosecuted for helping terminally ill loved ones die in most cases, and in recent months a series of public figures including Ian McEwan, Chris Broad and Sir Terry Pratchett have spoken out in favour of the law being relaxed still further.

But charities and groups supporting disabled people and the elderly fear that any change in the law would leave them feeling under pressure to end their lives.

In an article published on BMJ.com on Friday, Mr Fitzpatrick wrote: 'Disabled people, like others, and often with more reason, need to feel safe. Thus eroding what may already be a shaky sense of safety in medical care poses a further threat to disabled people's wellbeing, continuing care, and life itself.'

He cited the experience of Baroness Campbell of Surbiton, the disabled founder of Not Dead Yet, who was once told by doctors that they 'presumed' she wouldn't want resuscitation if she experienced complications during treatment.

'Very scared, she stayed awake in hospital for more than 48 hours.'

Mr Fitzpatrick said: 'The doctors' judgement, based on the idea of a 'life not worth living', is a moral judgement not of facts (medical or otherwise).

'A law permitting euthanasia would reinforce this position, further clearing the ground to take away lives based on a moral judgement rather than medical fact. The threat will extend to the lives of older, disabled people too.'

He mentioned the comments of Lord McColl made in the House of Lords that in the Netherlands, where euthanasia has been officially legalised and regulated since 2002, doctors found the cases increasingly easy to carry out while 'many elderly people in the Netherlands are so fearful of euthanasia that they carry cards around with them saying that they do not want it'.

This was a reference to the Dutch Patients' Association (NPV), which has 70,000 members of whom at least 6,000 have 'living will declarations' stating that they do not want euthanasia if they are taken into hospital or a nursing home.

Other Dutch people, however, make written declarations of their 'will to die'.

Mr Fitzpatrick concluded: 'These discussions are complex, involving deep moral questions that cannot and must not be treated as though they were merely matters of fact with clear and obvious answers that everyone must share, as though logic dictated it.

'The lives of many disabled people depend on resisting attempts to introduce a law legalising the intentional act of killing.'

21 April 2011

THE TELEGRAPH

Majority would support more compassionate euthanasia legislation

There is substantial public support for legalising assisted suicide in some form, a recent poll conducted on behalf of the Daily Telegraph suggests.

The survey found that a large majority (75%) of the British population think that legislation on euthanasia should be amended to allow some degree of assisted suicide. Just over two-thirds (67%) think that doctors in particular should have the legal power to end the life of a terminally-ill patient who has personally given a clear indication of wanting to die.

Taken to trial

This comes as the Director of Public Prosecutions in the United Kingdom, Keir Starmer, defended both the trial and recent acquittal of Kay Gilderdale, mother of the late Lynn Gilderdale. Lynn was a long-time sufferer of ME, and having had the chronic fatigue syndrome since the age of 14, she persuaded her mother to end her life out of compassion.

Starmer claimed that it was in the 'public interest' to bring the Gilderdale case to court, despite controversially declaring in September of last year that under certain circumstances, those assisting suicide will not be prosecuted. At the time, Starmer was heavily criticised by many areas of the public, including several pro-life lobbies, for his explicit statement that in certain cases, the flouting of assisted suicide laws would go unpunished.

Change in public opinion

However, in the wake of Gilderdale's trial, it seems public opinion is turning. Starmer has been heavily criticised for his decision to take the case to court at all, and 82% now agree that his concession to the Gilderdale case in September suggests a humane and sensible attitude towards assisted suicide – in contrast to the earlier case of Frances Inglis, who is serving life for ending the life of her brain-damaged son.

Indeed, that three-quarters of the public would support a change to euthanasia legislation suggests that most think a more compassionate approach should be embedded in the law.

8 February 2010

⇨ The above information is reprinted with kind permission from YouGov. Visit http://today.yougov.co.uk for more information.

© YouGov

Suicide drugs 'could be made available over the counter'

Suicide drugs could be made available from pharmacists if assisted dying was legalised, two of Britain's most highly regarded legal and medical experts have claimed.

Changing the law could make it possible for nurses and chemists to prescribe medication to sick and disabled patients which would enable them to kill themselves, according to a report by Lord Carlile and Baroness Finlay.

In the paper commissioned by the pressure group Living and Dying Well they also warned that liberalising euthanasia regulations could lead to state agencies being set up to decide whether or not people should be helped to die.

Lord Carlile is the Government-appointed independent assessor of terror legislation while Lady Finlay is Professor of Palliative Care at Cardiff University.

Their analysis warned that desperate patients and their families could resort to 'doctor shopping' in a bid to find a GP to help them die.

The report said: 'There is no reason why, if assisted dying were ever to be legalised, lethal drugs could not be prescribed by a physician, nurse or pharmacist.'

Although assisting a suicide carries a prison sentence of 14 years in Britain, more than 150 Britons have travelled to Zurich to die in the Dignitas suicide clinic in Switzerland in order to protect family members and friends from being charged with a crime.

Although two attempts to change the law in Britain have failed, the Government is under increasing pressure to support a right-to-die law.

5 May 2011

© Telegraph Media Group Limited 2011

YOUGOV / THE TELEGRAPH

Advance decisions

This article explains what an advance decision is, what it can and cannot do and also provides practical advice.

People who have dementia, or who are worried that they may develop it in future, are often concerned about how decisions about their medical treatment would be made if they lost the ability to decide for themselves. They may fear that they would be forced to receive life-sustaining or life-prolonging treatments long after they were able to achieve an acceptable or tolerable level of recovery, length of life or quality of life.

An advance statement would not bind healthcare professionals to a particular course of action if it conflicted with their professional judgement

The Mental Capacity Act 2005 gives people in England and Wales a statutory right to refuse treatment through an 'advance decision'. An advance decision allows a person to state what forms of treatment they would or would not like should they become unable to decide for themselves in the future.

Definitions of terms

An advance decision is intended to be a binding refusal of certain kinds of treatment as specified by the person making the advance decision.

An advance statement is a statement of general beliefs and aspects of life that a person values. It may reflect individual aspirations and preferences, and is sometimes called a 'personal values history'. The statement can be used to help health professionals and others, such as family members, to decide what sort of treatment the person would want if they were unable to communicate their wishes. However, an advance statement would not bind healthcare professionals to a particular course of action if it conflicted with their professional judgement.

An analgesic is a remedy that relieves or allays pain.

Capacity or competence is defined as the ability to understand the implications of a decision. A person is deemed to have capacity or competence if he or she:

⇨ can understand and retain information relevant to the decision in question (the definition of 'to retain information' has to be assessed on an individual basis);

⇨ can reflect on that information to arrive at a choice and use that information as part of the decision-making process;

⇨ can then express or otherwise communicate that choice.

A person diagnosed with dementia does not necessarily lack capacity. However, for people with dementia the loss of the ability to make informed decisions may be a gradual process, so the point at which they are no longer able to make a decision is quite difficult to pinpoint. Also, at some times a person may be quite capable of making their own decisions while at others their dementia can significantly affect their capacity and abilities. If a person's capacity fluctuates or is temporary, an assessment of the person's capacity must be made at the time the decision has to be made.

Cardiopulmonary resuscitation is a method of artificially restarting a person's heart.

A health and welfare attorney appointed under a Lasting Power of Attorney is an individual nominated and registered to make decisions on behalf of another person should that person lose capacity.

What are the advantages of deciding in advance?

Creating an advance decision and/or advance statement can bring some reassurance to a person worried about their future healthcare. When healthcare professionals are faced with difficult decisions about what treatment or care to give, an advance decision or advance statement will provide the best possible guide, and will help to ensure that the person's wishes are taken into account.

Preparing an advance decision or advance statement can open up a dialogue with doctors and nurses that might otherwise be delayed until it is too late. The process can also stimulate conversation with family and close friends, relieving them of some of the burden of decision making at what can be a distressing time.

Alzheimer's Society supports the idea of advance decisions, because they enable people with dementia to have a say in their future care. The British Medical Association supports the principle of advance decisions, and recognises that healthcare professionals may be legally liable if they disregard the contents of a valid advance decision.

ALZHEIMER'S SOCIETY

Are advance decisions legally enforceable?

As long as an advance decision is valid and applicable, it is legally enforceable in England and Wales.

⇨ Valid – the person who drew up the advance decision must have had mental capacity to do so at the time.

⇨ Applicable – the wording of the advance decision has to be relevant to the medical circumstances. If the wording is vague or there is a concern that the person was not referring to medical conditions and/or practices that they are actually experiencing, then the advance decision may not influence the doctors' decisions at all.

The advance decision must also:

⇨ be clear and unambiguous;

⇨ have been made when the person was over the age of 18 years, had sufficient mental capacity and been fully informed about the consequences of refusal of treatment, including the fact that it may hasten death;

⇨ have been intended to apply in the situation which has arisen;

⇨ not have been drawn up under the influence of other people.

If a health and welfare attorney has been appointed under a Lasting Power of Attorney, the health and welfare attorney should also be involved in discussions about the person's treatment, and healthcare professionals should take information provided by him or her into account. An advance decision overrides a Lasting Power of Attorney, unless a Lasting Power of Attorney prepared after the advance decision specifically confers authority on the attorney.

What an advance decision cannot do

An advance decision cannot be used to:

⇨ refuse treatment if the person has capacity to give or refuse consent to it;

⇨ refuse basic nursing care essential to keep a person comfortable, such as washing, bathing and mouth care;

An advance statement is a statement of general beliefs and aspects of life that a person values

⇨ refuse the offer of food or drink by mouth;

⇨ refuse the use of measures solely designed to maintain comfort – for example, painkillers;

⇨ demand treatment that a healthcare team considers inappropriate;

⇨ refuse treatment for mental disorder if the person is or is liable to be detained under the Mental Health Act 1983;

⇨ ask for anything that is against the law, such as euthanasia or assisting someone in taking their own life.

⇨ The above information is reprinted with kind permission from Alzheimer's Society. Visit www.alzheimers.org.uk for more information.

© Alzheimer's Society

End-of-life care survey

As new End-of-Life Rights Information Line is launched, survey finds that although a majority would want only comfort care at the end of life only 3% had made their wishes known in an advance decision.

A poll commissioned by Compassion in Dying found that six out of ten adults (60%) would only want comfort care at the end of their lives, although just 3% had made their treatment wishes clear in an advance decision. Fewer than two in ten people (14%) would want limited medical intervention – with less than one in ten (8%) people wanting full medical intervention at the end of life.

The majority (53%) also wrongly believed that they had the legal right to make treatment decisions on behalf of their loved ones, if their loved ones lost the ability to communicate their wishes.

Today (19 May), as part of Dying Matters Week, Compassion in Dying, a national charity focussed on end of life rights, is launching a new phone line dedicated to informing people about their existing legal rights and supporting them in ensuring their end-of-life wishes are respected.

The results of this poll highlight the need for people to be better informed about their legal rights at the end of life, so that the medical treatment wishes they express are respected.

Dr Richard Scheffer, retired consultant in palliative medicine and medical director of an independent hospice, said:

'I think this poll result will come as a surprise to many people. There is often an assumption that we must do all we can to keep people alive. However, when someone is dying, it is often in their best interest for medical staff to focus on using palliative treatments to ensure they are comfortable rather than to continue more aggressive life-sustaining treatment. This poll shows that a majority of the public shares this view. Ultimately, what an individual wants at the end of life is of the utmost importance.

'People clearly have preferences about what treatment they do or don't want once they know that they're dying, but few people have made those preferences clear in advance decision documents. People often believe that decisions about their treatment can be made on their behalf by family or friends, while the reality is that in the absence of an advance decision or Lasting Power of Attorney (LPA), these decisions are made by healthcare professionals. Doctors or nurses will consult family members, but ultimately it is the healthcare team who must decide what they believe to be in the best interests of the patient – and that may not always be the treatment the patient would have chosen.

'I am delighted to be able to support the formation of an information line on end-of-life rights. I believe the phone line will be of enormous help and support to patients facing their own deaths and also to loved ones trying to ensure that those they care for most have the best treatment at the end of life, based on their own wishes.'

As well as the new End-of-Life Rights Information Line, Compassion in Dying also provides free advance decisions, guides to rights at the end of life for the general public, and toolkits for medical professionals on how advance decisions can be integrated into their patients' care.

19 May 2011

⇨ The above information is reprinted with kind permission from Compassion in Dying. Visit www.compassionindying.org.uk for more information.

© Compassion in Dying

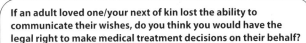

If an adult loved one/your next of kin lost the ability to communicate their wishes, do you think you would have the legal right to make medical treatment decisions on their behalf?

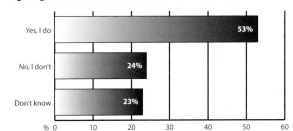

Do you currently have an advance decision* document?

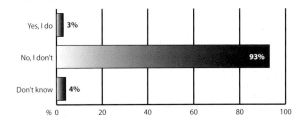

*An advance decision is a document that allows you to set out your wishes and preferences for medical treatment in advance, in the event that you become unable to communicate with your healthcare team. The refusal of medical treatment, including life-prolonging treatment, is legally binding with an advance decision.

Source: YouGov poll on awareness of end-of-life rights, April 2011, Commissioned by Compassion in Dying. © YouGov (www.yougov.com)

COMPASSION IN DYING

'The law is a mess'

In a frank interview with ePolitix.com, James Harris, Head of Campaigns and Communications at Dignity in Dying, outlines why a change in the law on assisted dying is necessary.

Dignity in Dying campaigns for assisted dying, not assisted suicide or euthanasia: what is the difference?

Dignity in Dying advocates assisted dying – this gives terminally ill, mentally competent adults the choice to control the time and manner of their own death via life-ending medication, within safeguards. We do not advocate assisted suicide for non-terminally ill people. Furthermore, we do not advocate euthanasia which allows doctors to directly end patients' lives.

This isn't just a theoretical difference, each of these practices exists today: assisted suicide in Switzerland; voluntary euthanasia in Belgium, Luxembourg and the Netherlands; and assisted dying in the US states of Oregon and Washington. Dignity in Dying believes that assisted dying provides patients with a choice to end unnecessary suffering at the end of life, whilst providing an important built-in safeguard to ensure that the final decision lies solely with the person asking for help to die, because it is the patient and not the doctor who administers the life-ending medication.

People should have choice and control at the end of life if they consider their suffering unbearable, so long as people are also protected against coercion or abuse. We believe that the law can be changed to remove a duty to suffer from some people without creating a duty to die for others.

Do you think if there was a marked improvement in end-of-life care, assisted dying would not be needed?

No. Palliative care can help to ensure that most people have a dignified death, but not all. Palliative care providers acknowledge that for some people, palliative care is not enough to alleviate suffering at the end of life. This should not be a case of either/or. Everyone should be able to access good quality end-of-life care in their preferred setting where possible, but we should not turn our backs on those who, despite access to such care, consider their suffering to be unbearable. Doing so results in terminally ill people attempting to end their lives without advice or support, often alone, and sometimes in a foreign country.

Do you often come across the so-called 'postcode lottery' when you look at the quality of end-of-life care?

Sadly yes, there are well-recognised barriers to accessing good quality care, not just based on postcode but also on diagnosis. Tremendous effort, for example, has been put into caring for those with terminal cancer, but although great progress is being made, less attention has been paid to those suffering with pulmonary and neurological terminal conditions. Whilst Britain has led the world in palliative care provision, our hospices have evolved outside of the NHS. We need to ensure that the level of care and expertise they provide is replicated through every care setting where people die. Valuable work is being done via the National End of Life Care Programme and progress is being made, but we must not accept less than the best when it comes to end-of-life care – dealing with a loved one's death is difficult enough, but it is compounded beyond words if they die without dignity.

What is your opinion on the Health Bill: do you think this will have a positive effect on things like the postcode lottery?

I have my concerns, as do others. The chair of the BMA's GP committee, Laurence Buckman, recently warned that the Health Bill could lead to the poor, elderly, infirm and terminally ill losing out to 'internal medical tourists'. Personally, I struggle to see how the postcode lottery can be eradicated without pressure being exerted from

the top and enforced via ring-fenced budgets. That said, the Government has exerted a lot of political capital on these reforms and they will be only too aware that the electorate won't tolerate the end of the NHS as we know it. So they must be confident that they have got it right. We must strive to ensure that the necessary checks and balances are in place to make sure that there is uniformity in the provision of end-of-life care amongst the new GP consortia responsible for commissioning.

Do you think a change in the law around assisted dying is the only way of ensuring protection for vulnerable people at the end of their life?

To be frank, the law is a mess. It is legal for a doctor, with little to no safeguards, to sedate a patient and remove artificial hydration and nutrition, with only one outcome: their patient's death. It is also legal for a doctor, with little to no safeguards, to administer pain relief in sufficient quantities to end a patient's life, as long as bringing about their patient's death is not their intention. In addition to existing clinical practice which circumnavigates assistance to die, the law which prohibits professional assistance to die, in effect, forgives compassionate, amateur assistance to die.

An assisted dying law, with safeguards and defined criteria, would provide a better-regulated and patient-centred approach to end-of-life decision making. It would allow terminally ill, mentally competent adults, who consider their suffering unbearable despite access to good quality end-of-life care, choice and control over their death without having to resort to travelling abroad to die or attempting to take their life at home. Critically, rather than relying on an investigation and possible (but unlikely) prosecution after someone has died to deter abuse (which someone once said to me requires an 'autopsy of the soul'), a change in the law would allow for a full consideration of someone's request to die when they are still alive, and alternative options could be set out.

So yes, not only would a change in the law allow for greater patient choice, it would also provide greater patient protection.

If there was a vote in the House of Commons on the issue, do you think it should be a free vote as it is a matter of conscience?

Yes. This is not a party political issue – there are supporters and opponents of change in all of the main parties. However, I would like to see all candidates during general elections openly set out how they would be likely to vote on this and other issues of conscience so that people can make up their minds accordingly. I

would define myself as socially liberal, but I don't think that one party has a monopoly on that front. Perhaps alongside party manifestos we need candidates to issue personal manifestos. There are some politicians who oppose a change in the law on assisted dying whom I greatly respect for their views on other issues. However, given the importance I personally attach to this issue, I would struggle to vote for them.

Do you think some MPs do not want to meddle with the status quo when it comes to assisted dying?

It can't be easy. Given the vocal support and opposition to a change in the law, there must be an element of 'damned if they do, and damned if they don't'. Yet there are consequences for society of doing nothing to change a law that is now 50 years old and is demonstrably no longer fit for purpose. I would simply ask MPs to reflect on what they would want for themselves and their loved ones at the end of life. If they would want choice, why would they deny that to others?

2 February 2011

⇨ The above information is reprinted with kind permission from ePolitix.com. Visit www.epolitix.com for more information.

© ePolitix.com

Assisting a suicide is a criminal offence punishable by 14 years in prison. Do you believe the law on assisted suicide should...

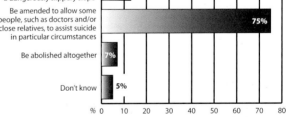

The Director of Public Prosecutions (DPP) has signalled that although assisted suicide remains a criminal offence he will not prosecute relatives who assist in the suicide of a relative or close friend with a 'clear, settled and informed' wish to die. As long as the law remains unchanged, do you agree with this approach?

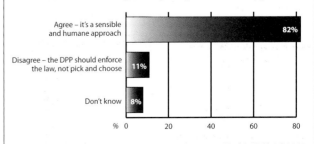

Sample Size: 2053 GB adults. Fieldwork: 26-28 January 2010. Source: YouGov (www.yougov.com)

⇨ Euthanasia comes from Greek, meaning 'pleasant death'. It typically refers to the killing of a person for their own (or another) good, usually to end their suffering. (page 1)

⇨ The ongoing campaigns to legalise euthanasia or assisted dying, some of which are attracting the support of various celebrities, have raised particular concerns amongst people with disabilities and their families and supporters. (page 2)

⇨ The 'slippery slope' or 'thin end of the wedge' argument says that if you permit voluntary euthanasia, involuntary euthanasia will follow. (page 5)

⇨ When the doctor prescribes a fatal potion or administers a lethal injection, rather than battling to save you from disease and/or death, trust in doctor–patient relationships risks being destroyed. (page 8)

⇨ In Oregon, whilst numbers of assisted suicide have risen since legalisation, overall numbers have remained low (under 0.2% of all deaths) and the kinds of people being helped to die have not changed. (page 11)

⇨ Under English law, all adults have the right to refuse medical treatment, even if that treatment is required to save their life, as long as they have sufficient capacity (the ability to use and understand information to make a decision). (page 13)

⇨ There is now a consensus on the issue that high quality palliative care should be made available to all patients at the end of their lives, regardless of their medical condition, age, ethnicity or location. (page 16)

⇨ Some 70 per cent of disabled people would be concerned if the law on assisted suicide were to change because they feel it would lead to pressure being placed on disabled people to end their lives, a Scope-commissioned ComRes survey has shown. (page 19)

⇨ A review of research carried out over 20 years suggests that UK doctors appear to consistently oppose euthanasia and physician-assisted suicide (PAS). The findings highlight a gap between doctors' attitudes and those of the UK public. (page 22)

⇨ Deliberately and directly taking the life of another person, whether that person is dying or not, constitutes the crime of murder. The Suicide Act 1961, updated by the Coroners and Justice Act 2009, makes encouraging or assisting a suicide a crime punishable by up to 14 years' imprisonment. (page 24)

⇨ The Scottish Parliament voted on 1st December 2010 to throw out the End of Life Assistance (Scotland) Bill which proposed to legalise assisted suicide and euthanasia in Scotland. (page 30)

⇨ The doctor–patient relationship is one founded primarily on trust and opponents to a change in the law argue that by taking on the additional role of assisted dying, trust could be lost and the doctor–patient relationship damaged. (page 31)

⇨ Elderly people in the Netherlands are so fearful of being killed by doctors that they carry cards saying they do not want euthanasia, according to a campaigner who says allowing assisted suicide in Britain would put the vulnerable at risk. (page 33)

⇨ One survey found that a large majority (75%) of the British population think that legislation on euthanasia should be amended to allow some degree of assisted suicide. Just over two-thirds (67%) think that doctors in particular should have the legal power to end the life of a terminally-ill patient who has personally given a clear indication of wanting to die. (page 34)

⇨ An advance decision allows a person to state what forms of treatment they would or would not like should they become unable to decide for themselves in the future. (page 35)

⇨ Six out of ten adults (60%) would only want comfort care at the end of their lives, although just 3% had made their treatment wishes clear in an advance decision. (page 37)

Advance decision

Sometimes referred to as 'living wills', advanced decisions are legal statements outlining a patients' wishes with regards to their medical treatment should they not be able to make decisions or communicate their wishes at a later stage. Advanced decisions can include the request for life-sustaining or life-prolonging treatments, as well as the refusal of treatments.

Assisted suicide

Aiding somebody to take their own life. This is illegal in the UK.

Autonomy

The ability to make independent, informed decisions, free from coercion or outside influences. It is sometimes argued that patients should have greater autonomy over their medical treatment and the freedom to choose euthanasia if they wish.

Dignitas clinic

A clinic in Switzerland which assists terminally-ill patients to end their lives. Non-medical assisted suicide is legal in Switzerland and terminally-ill patients from other countries sometimes travel to the clinic specifically to end their lives. This is sometimes referred to as 'death tourism'.

Double effect

The principle of double effect refers to a treatment prescribed by a doctor for the purpose of relieving pain or distressing symptoms, but which has the side-effect of shortening the patient's life. Although the doctor will be aware that the treatment will induce an early death, it is not considered euthanasia because the main reason for the prescription is pain relief.

DPP policy on assisted suicide

The 'Policy for Prosecutors in respect of Cases of Encouraging or Assisting Suicide' published in 2010 by the Director of Public Prosecutions, which clarifies that an act of assisted suicide motivated by compassion may not lead to prosecution for relatives of a terminally-ill patient.

Involuntary euthanasia

Intentionally ending a patient's life without their consent.

Even if the act of euthanasia is motivated by compassion it is still considered involuntary euthanasia if the patient in question is unable to give informed consent.

Palliative care

A specialist area of care which provides relief from pain but does not cure a disease or illness. It is often administered to patients suffering from terminal illnesses in order to improve their quality of life before they die.

Palliative sedation

The sedation of a terminally-ill patient in order to relieve suffering and pain. This option is considered a last resort and is only used in the final moments of a patient's life.

Physician-assisted suicide (PAS)

A doctor prescribing lethal drugs in order that a patient may take their own life is known as physician-assisted suicide.

Sanctity of life

A term usually associated with religious faiths, particularly Christianity, which refers to the idea that all life is sacred as created by God, and no human being has the right to end a life.

'Slippery slope' argument

One of the principle arguments given by anti-euthanasia groups and individuals. The 'slippery slope' argument suggests that if a Government were to legalise voluntary euthanasia, a change in citizens' and healthcare professionals' attitudes would eventually result in implications such as involuntary euthanasia, pressure on very ill or disabled people to end their lives prematurely and a decline in the importance placed on palliative care.

Terminal illness

An illness for which there is no cure and which will ultimately bring about the patient's death.

Voluntary euthanasia

Intentionally ending the life of a patient who has previously given their consent for euthanasia. It is usually requested by patients who are suffering from a terminal illness and who wish to end their pain and suffering.

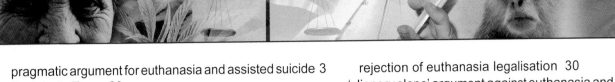

ACKNOWLEDGEMENTS

The publisher is grateful for permission to reproduce the following material.

While every care has been taken to trace and acknowledge copyright, the publisher tenders its apology for any accidental infringement or where copyright has proved untraceable. The publisher would be pleased to come to a suitable arrangement in any such case with the rightful owner.

Chapter One: The Ethical Debate

Euthanasia, © Politics.co.uk, Arguments for and against euthanasia, © Crown copyright is reproduced with the permission of Her Majesty's Stationery Office, A humanist discussion of euthanasia, © British Humanist Association, Assisted suicide: how the chattering classes have got it wrong, © Centre for Policy Studies, The slippery slope argument, © World Federation of Right to Die Societies, Brief answers to five objections, © South Australian Euthanasia Society (SAVES), Need for change, © Healthcare Professionals for Assisted Dying, Alternatives to euthanasia and assisted suicide, © Crown copyright is reproduced with the permission of Her Majesty's Stationery Office, What is the relationship between assisted suicide and dying and palliative care?, © Demos, End-of-life issues and palliative care, © Scottish Churches Parliamentary Office, Poll shows disabled people's fears over assisted suicide, © Scope, Terry Pratchett defends Choosing to Die documentary from critics, © Guardian News and Media Limited, Whose right is it anyway?, © Disability Now, UK doctors consistently oppose euthanasia and assisted suicide, © SAGE Publications, Support grows for 'right to die', © YouGov.

Chapter Two: Legal Issues and Implications

Assisted dying and the status quo, © Demos, Legislation is not the answer for assisted suicide, © Politics.co.uk, We need an assisted dying law, © Guardian News and Media Limited, Scottish Parliament rejects Bill to legalise euthanasia, © CARE, Impact on the medical profession and doctor–patient relationships, © Demos, Belgian patients are being killed without their consent, © The Christian Institute, Fearful elderly people carry 'anti-euthanasia cards', © Telegraph Media Group Limited, Majority would support more compassionate euthanasia legislation, © YouGov, Suicide drugs 'could be made available over the counter', © Telegraph Media Group Limited, Advance decisions, © Alzheimer's Society, End-of-life care survey, © Compassion in Dying, 'The law is a mess', © ePolitix.

Illustrations

Pages 4, 21, 27, 31: Angelo Madrid; pages 10, 12, 22, 38: Don Hatcher; pages 11, 23, 30, 36: Simon Kneebone; pages 15, 26: Bev Aisbett.

Cover photography

Left: © Hotels in Eastbourne: www.eastbourneguide.com. Centre: © Jean Carneiro. Right: © Pawel Kryj.

Additional acknowledgements

Editorial by Carolyn Kirby on behalf of Independence.

And with thanks to the Independence team: Mary Chapman, Sandra Dennis and Jan Sunderland.

Lisa Firth
Cambridge
September, 2011

ASSIGNMENTS

The following tasks aim to help you think through the issues surrounding the euthanasia debate and provide a better understanding of the topic.

1 Write a short paragraph defining euthanasia. Explain the difference between voluntary and involuntary euthanasia, physician-assisted suicide and assisted suicide (non-medical).

2 Using newspapers and the Internet, carry out your own research into a legal case which has influenced public opinion and/or the law with regards to the euthanasia debate: for example, the cases of Diane Pretty or Debbie Purdy. What did those seeking a change in the law hope to achieve, and why? What conclusion did the courts reach? Do you agree with the conclusion? Write a summary of your findings.

3 Read *Assisted suicide: how the chattering classes have got it wrong* on page 7. In the article, the author argues that a change in the assisted suicide law will 'risk having a strident elite condemning the less fortunate to a premature death'. To what extent do you agree with this statement? Discuss the writer's assertion in groups of four.

4 Imagine your local MP is campaigning for a change in the law which would legalise assisted suicide in the UK. Write a letter to your MP expressing your views on the topic – would you support or oppose their proposals? Support your argument using facts, case studies and statistics.

5 Read the play 'Ghosts' by Henrik Ibsen. What decision do you think Helen Alving should make: should she end her son Oswald's life in accordance with his wishes? Write a summary of the play and a brief review.

6 Is voluntary euthanasia legal in the UK? Briefly summarise what you know about the law surrounding euthanasia. Include information on the DPP assisted suicide policy.

7 Imagine you work for a charity which campaigns on behalf of severely disabled people. Write a press release for your charity's website explaining how a change in the UK's euthanasia law might adversely affect the people your charity represents. How might it make those people feel? How would your charity respond?

8 Some people who have been diagnosed with terminal illnesses choose to end their lives at the Dignitas clinic in Switzerland, where non-medical assisted suicide is legal. However, due to their illness, they often need help travelling to the clinic. Should their relatives be legally allowed to assist them with this journey? Or is this the same as condoning assisted suicide? Debate this controversial issue in pairs.

9 Study the table on page 28, 'Jurisdictions in which some form of assisted suicide is legal'. Choose one jurisdiction from the list and carry out your own research into the details of their assisted suicide or euthanasia legislation. Try to find some statistics on how many acts of euthanasia or assisted suicide take place each year within this region. Why was the law changed to allow euthanasia or assisted suicide in this area? Summarise your research findings in a concise article.

10 Watch Terry Pratchett's documentary 'Choosing to Die'. Do you think the BBC were right to show the death of a terminally-ill patient? Write a review of the programme.

11 The World Federation of Right to Die Societies consists of 45 pro-euthanasia organisations from around the world. Visit their website at www.worldrtd.net to find out more about the Federation. When were they established? What work do they do? Write a summary of your findings.

12 Watch the film 'Million Dollar Baby' (warning: some may find the plot of this film harrowing). What questions does the film raise surrounding the euthanasia debate? Write a review.

13 'This house believes that it would never be acceptable for a doctor to help someone to die, as this is medically unethical, in breach of the Hippocratic Oath and it would erode the trust between doctor and patient.' Debate this motion in two groups, with one arguing in favour and the other against.